Effective Investing

Every owner of a physical copy of this edition of

Effective Investing

can download the eBook for free direct from us at Harriman House, in a DRM-free format that can be read on any eReader, tablet or smartphone.

Simply head to:

ebooks.harriman-house.com/effectiveinvesting

to get your copy now.

Effective Investing

A simple way to build wealth by investing in funds

Mark Dampier

HARRIMAN HOUSE LTD
18 College Street
Petersfield
Hampshire
GU31 4AD
GREAT BRITAIN
Tel: +44 (0)1730 233870

Email: **enquiries@harriman-house.com**
Website: **www.harriman-house.com**

First published in Great Britain in 2015.

Paperback ISBN: 978-0-85719-467-1
eBook ISBN: 978-0-85719-511-1

British Library Cataloguing in Publication Data
A CIP catalogue record for this book can be obtained from the British Library.

CONTENTS

ABOUT THE AUTHOR   vi

CHAPTER 1. **Introduction**   1

CHAPTER 2. **The Basics of Investing**   12

CHAPTER 3. **Getting Started**   39

CHAPTER 4. **Narrowing the Field**   55

CHAPTER 5. **How to Pick the Best Funds**   71

CHAPTER 6. **Building and Managing Your Portfolio**   112

CHAPTER 7. **How I Invest My Own Money**   139

CHAPTER 8. **Other Ways to Invest**   171

CHAPTER 9. **Reflections on a Three-Decade Career**   195

CHAPTER 10. **Final Thoughts**   227

ACKNOWLEDGEMENTS   229

APPENDICES   232

INDEX   246

ABOUT THE AUTHOR

Mark Dampier has been head of research at Hargreaves Lansdown, the UK's largest independent stockbroking firm, since 1998. He has been in the financial services industry for 32 years, initially working as an advisor helping individual clients to invest their money. He holds a BA Honours degree in Law. Mark has become one of the best-known and most widely quoted figures in the fund management industry. He writes a weekly column in the *Independent* on funds and markets and regularly comments in the national press and on broadcast media. This is his first book (and, he swears, definitely his last!). In his spare time, depending on the season, you will find him shooting, skiing, sailing or fishing.

CHAPTER 1.
Introduction

"Where should I invest my money?"

I HAVE LOST COUNT OF THE NUMBER OF TIMES THAT I HAVE BEEN asked this question over the years. It certainly runs into the tens of thousands. I think my mother was probably the first, more than 40 years ago. Today, as head of research for the UK's largest fund and stockbroking firm, my job is to help find answers to that question for more than 730,000 clients.

It is clear to me that there is more demand than ever for help in making good investment decisions. One reason I hear almost every time I meet a new client is that he or she has had a bad experience at the hands of banks and other traditional financial services providers. I find it hard to think of any businesses that have done more over the years to alienate their customer base than the big banks and insurance companies.

A succession of scandals, fines and rip-off practices means that most people no longer trust the institutions they would ordinarily have committed their money to in the past. Even if you can afford a financial advisor or wealth manager, it is far from certain that you will find the experience worth the money. The best advisors are very good: but not everyone finds it a rewarding experience.

People today rightly want better results, better service and a greater say in how their money is managed. Fortunately in the last ten years technology has moved on so rapidly that the dream of controlling your own investments has become a practical possibility for almost everyone. The development of online investment platforms – one-stop websites that enable you to take full control over all your money – is revolutionising the way that money is saved and invested. You will be hearing more about platforms in this book; they are a game-changer for anyone looking to take greater control over their own finances.

A second reason DIY investing is on the increase stems from the generous tax incentives for investors that governments have introduced over the past 20 years. These make it both easier and potentially more rewarding than before for private individuals to look after their own money. The availability of tax wrappers such as ISAs or SIPPs (DIY pension funds), plus annual capital gains allowances, mean that most people can invest many thousands of pounds a year without having to pay any tax on their gains. The advantages of saving into ISAs and pensions are so great that I urge everybody to take advantage when they can.

In this brave new world, inevitably there is growing demand for well-researched, independent information and advice. If you are looking at this book, the chances are that you are one of those looking for help. My hope is that you will find much of value in the pages that follow. The aim is to share with you, in plain language, the most important things that I have learnt about investing over the nearly 35 years that I have been working in the field. I believe that anyone can make money from investing if they have the right knowledge and help.

What to expect

Like anything in life, you need to put in some work and research to try and get the best out of investing. My book is not intended as a 'how to' manual or reference book. There are plenty of those out there and nowadays you can Google so much. It is rather an attempt to give some practical pointers and the fruits of my own experience, including my past mistakes. Whenever possible, I have concentrated on setting out broad principles rather than getting bogged down in technical details, which in my experience can easily deter the reader. If you come across a term that you don't understand, it is very easy to look up the definition on the internet. I have added some useful links in the appendices.

Taking control over your personal finances is bound to play an increasing role in most people's lives as the state rolls back. Governments simply can't afford to provide everything they once promised their citizens, such as long-term care, inflation-linked retirement benefits and universal healthcare. Not for nothing has the UK recently launched an auto-enrolment scheme to make sure that all employees pay into a pension. How well your investments perform could well make the difference between your having a fun retirement or a dreary one with little money. Investment isn't boring unless you believe that making money and providing for your future are unimportant. I hope this book might prove to be a stepping stone on that journey.

My hope is that you will be sufficiently energised by what I have to say to not only start investing, but to find out more for yourself. The fact that investment appears to be such a complicated business is probably one of the reasons UK investors have traditionally turned to property instead – something they can see, feel and touch and has historically been very profitable. However, property is not without its problems. Few property fans seem to dwell on such things as bad tenants, tenancy voids, maintenance problems and repairs. Dealing with all these things has always struck me as far more complicated and stressful than buying an investment fund.

Investing in funds has been my particular area of professional expertise for many years. I explain why you should think about going down the same route in chapter 3. Picking individual shares, which is an alternative approach, requires a different set of skills and in my experience is a more time-consuming and difficult route to follow. Please don't let me put you off trying direct investing in shares, however. I just happen to believe that funds are the simplest and most convenient way to invest money, whatever your ultimate purpose may be – be that a pension, a house, a holiday, a family wedding or just personal enthusiasm. It is how I invest my money and also the way that most individual investors do in practice choose to invest.

The order of content is as follows. First, I look at the basic principles of investing and explain how I think ordinary investors should think about what they are aiming to do. Then I go on to outline the range and types of funds that are available to individual investors and explain why you should look carefully at using a platform to research and execute your investment choices. I also summarise the tax breaks that the government, in its wisdom, offers you as a potential investor. (I know putting the words 'government' and 'wisdom' close to each other is a bit of a liberty, but these tax-saving benefits, unlike much else that is presented as government largesse, are real.)

Next I describe some basic steps that will help you choose the best investment funds and combine them to create a well-balanced portfolio. I summarise what is in a range of starter portfolios I have designed you to help you get started, depending on your appetite for risk. I go on to explain in detail how I invest my own money, with a description of all the largest individual holdings. Then I cover some of the practical issues that arise from the need to monitor and account for your investments. The next chapter explains my thoughts about some other options for investors, including so-called passive funds, investment trusts and buy-to-let property. The concluding chapter sums up the most relevant lessons that I feel I have learnt over the course of my 35-year career.

Why listen to me?

Before getting into the meat of all this, you may want to know something about my qualifications for presuming to tell you how to become a successful self-directed investor (or DIY investor, for short). These days, you cannot set yourself up to give investment advice without formal qualifications and personal authorisation by the Financial Conduct Authority, the financial services industry regulator. Quite rightly I would not be allowed to do my job without those qualifications.

But you may also be reassured to know that most of what I know about the business of investing I learnt not from a textbook but from the university of life. The reason I know that anyone can become a successful investor without any prior knowledge is that I have travelled the full length of that road myself.

When I came into the industry for the first time, remarkable as it sounds, no formal qualifications were required. Most of the business was unregulated and sales-driven, frequently with disastrous consequences. I got my first job with a financial advisor for no other reason than that he happened to live next door to my mother in Teddington, Middlesex. I am still not quite sure what Kean Seager, the founder of Whitechurch Securities and the gentleman in question, saw in me. (I suspect the main attraction might have been that I was not only keen and interested in investment, but also cheap at the price!)

The little I knew about investing the day I started was hardly worth knowing. I did have a degree, but it was in a subject, law, that I found stultifyingly dull. After going to law college, I soon decided that spending 40 years doing conveyancing work, which seems to be the fate awaiting most lawyers of my ability, had little appeal. I was on the lookout for something more interesting. Investment turned out to be the answer, and it is a career choice I have never regretted.

Mind you, in those early years I knew what I most wanted to do, which was to spend as much time as possible on the ski slopes. Skiing was my main interest. On my CV it says I took a "double gap year" as a ski bum (because, to be frank, I enjoyed the first one so much). I had two years of pure pleasure and irresponsibility, something that I think every youngster should be encouraged to try before getting down to serious career work. But all good things have to come to an end, and after two seasons on the slopes and having recently become engaged, I was under pressure from both sets of parents to find a 'proper job'. The offer to work for Whitechurch Securities therefore came as a welcome lifeline at just the right time.

From bad times to good

As things turned out, I was fortunate to start in the investment business just as the UK was coming out of its worst economic crisis since the second world war. The 1970s had been a horrible time for savers and investors. Runaway inflation and penal tax rates had devastated the savings that many of my parents' generation had built up. The top rate of income tax was 83% from 1974 to 1979 and there was an additional tax of 15% to pay on dividends and other types of investment income. Exchange controls and an insidious regulation called the dollar premium made it both difficult and expensive to invest money overseas. The stock market fell by 75% from its peak in 1972 to its low point in 1975, and the chancellor of the exchequer, Denis Healey, had to go cap in hand to the International Monetary Fund, rather like Greece today, for a humiliating bailout.

It is hard for anyone who was not around then to imagine how bad it was. But although these miserable memories have faded, they were still very fresh in most people's minds the day I started work in 1983. I may not have known much about money, but I was very keen to find out more. I read all the specialist investment publications I could lay my hands on, and when I didn't know something (which was often), I would go and ask my boss. I was lucky that Kean was always happy to share his knowledge with me, as I try to do with those I work with today.

Having worked as the investment manager of a pension fund run by a bank, Kean knew his stuff and had recently set himself up as what today we would call a financial advisor, helping clients to invest their money and living off the commissions that their business generated. It was a good time to start, as this was still a period when most financial advisors were former life assurance salesmen. They may have had great charm and persistence but they knew almost nothing about investment itself. The competition was therefore none too demanding.

Although Kean initially expected to do most of his business helping to create portfolios of individual shares and bonds, it soon became clear that the best business opportunity was going to be in picking unit trusts (the first professionally managed investment funds to be specifically designed for the mass market). Although not as popular then as they are today, unit trusts had a number of advantages for both investors and their financial advisors. They were easy to buy and sell and, for the advisor, easier to scale up into a decent business, helped by the improving economic climate of the period.

As interest rates started to come down, and the economy and stock market began to recover through the 1980s, the business of creating, selling and distributing funds quickly turned into a growth industry and in turn became, as it remains, my personal area of specialism. The other popular product among advisors at that time was something called an investment bond, which were sold by life assurance companies (and paid even better commissions than unit trusts). Like endowments, which in those days many people invested in to help them repay their mortgages, they combined life insurance and an investment fund. The door-to-door salesmen who got people saving in those days were highly incentivised to flog them. However, as an investment option, investment bonds were not as good value as a plain unit trust.

After several years working and learning on the job at Whitechurch Securities, and an interlude working elsewhere, in 1998 I was persuaded to move across Bristol and join Hargreaves Lansdown, one of Whitechurch Securities' main rivals. The company had started life in 1981 as a two-man operation run from the back bedroom of Peter Hargreaves' house. By the time I arrived it was already a profitable and growing business, on its way to becoming the market-leading financial services business it is today. In little over 30 years, HL, as it is widely known, has grown from a small privately-owned company with a few hundred clients to one of the UK's 100 largest publicly-quoted businesses, with assets under management or administration of more than £55 billion. It has been quite a ride and one in which I have been fortunate to play a part.

What strikes me today is how lucky I was to find that the principles of sound investment which I had slowly learnt for myself by working with my original clients were also shared by the two founders of HL. That made it an easy transition for me. The very first client that I had at Whitechurch Securities was an ex-military man who was coming up to retirement. (I sometimes joked that I could have invaded a small country with the knowledge and expertise of my original client list, such was the preponderance of former officers and servicemen.) He told me that he needed to earn an income from his investments, but also wanted some scope to make a capital gain as well.

I did some research and put together a portfolio of the best equity income funds I could find at the time. Three decades later I continue to recommend exactly the same thing for many clients today, as equity income funds remain in my view, for reasons that I shall explain, one of the best building blocks for a wide range of investors, beginners and wealthy alike.

Simple, but not easy

Ben Graham is a famous American investor who, in the 1930s, wrote the first definitive book about picking shares. He was also one of the first to make the observation that the business of investing is "simple, but not easy". Although I have had to learn that lesson myself the hard way, it is very much the way I have come to see it too. The opportunity that investors have today to take greater control of their own financial destiny is a hugely exciting and positive development. The only shame is that so many people, while anxious or aware that they need to take a greater interest in how their money is doing, remain daunted by the apparent complexity of the task. It is nothing like as complicated as it sounds.

I hope to convince you that, while there are no shortcuts to investment success, making the effort can be rewarding. If a former ski bum like me can do it, so can you! Of course, it takes concentration and hard work. You have to be flexible and adapt your thinking to the prevailing climate, taking the rough with the smooth along the way. It is better to build your wealth steadily over a number of years rather than trying to chase instant returns. And yes, there are plenty of pitfalls lying in wait for the unwary. The good news, however, is that the rewards over longer periods of time will comfortably repay the effort.

CHAPTER 2.
The Basics
of Investing

WHAT IS THE OBJECTIVE OF INVESTING? MOST PEOPLE tend to say something like, "To make as much money as possible". My answer is different. As I see it, the objective of investing is to improve your quality of life. What you are doing when you start investing is making a conscious decision to put a certain amount of money aside in the reasoned belief that it will be worth more in the future – a little sacrifice today for a lot more gain tomorrow.

Successful investing is therefore a passport to a better life for your family. It is worth emphasising that you don't need to have huge sums ready and waiting. What you need is the discipline to save a little regularly. Over the years I have often been told that it was pointless to save small amounts each month; they could never amount to anything. But that is the first and biggest mistake you can make about investing. As we'll see, time can do wonders for the value of investments, no matter how small they start out.

Part of the reason for writing this book is my belief that the more confident you are that you can grow your money by investing, the more likely it is that you will in fact put aside money for that purpose, rather than spend it some other way. And the more committed you are with your investments, the less time it will take to arrive at any given financial objective. In a world where bank accounts pay virtually nothing in the way of interest, the one certainty is that unless you do invest your money profitably, it cannot grow in value and you are never going to improve your quality of life as much as you want.

You need to have a plan

Having decided that you want to improve the quality of your life in the future, where to start? In my view there is no avoiding having a financial plan, however basic. The clients we see at Hargreaves Lansdown come in all shapes and sizes. Some have more than £25m invested with us and own almost every kind of investment that exists. Others may be putting as little as £25 a month into a single savings scheme. As far as I am concerned, that doesn't make any difference: whoever you are, and whatever your circumstances, you still need to find the time to sit down and put together a sensible financial plan.

Such a plan involves working out:

- what money you have today

- what money you need now and in the future

- what you are trying to achieve over the course of your investing life.

Of course, other than death and taxation, nothing in life is ever certain. Everybody's circumstances are different. Some things can only be estimated very roughly and life expectancy is a lottery. But without the discipline of at least a rudimentary financial plan you cannot really hope to make effective investment decisions for the future. You wouldn't dream of setting off in a car without knowing where you are going and how long it might take. Managing your money is no different. Nearly everyone can do it – just as long as they are willing to make the effort.

The DIY approach

In my opinion, money spent getting professional help to put together a financial plan for your life is almost always money well-spent. It may cost you a few hundred pounds. People seem only to take financial advice when their personal circumstances change – such as after death, divorce or the arrival of children – but having a regular professional check-up every few years is sensible.

Nevertheless, it is not impossible to put together the rudiments of a financial plan yourself. A good financial plan does not need to be complicated. It is better to be roughly right than precisely wrong. But it does need to be thorough.

1. What you earn

The plan starts with the figures for what you and your family earn now, with a realistic assessment of how income from all sources might grow over the next few years, allowing for tax, national insurance and other deductions.

2. What you spend

The next step is to work out your outgoings, starting with essentials such as food, housing costs (mortgage or rent), utility bills and life insurance, followed by the amounts you spend on discretionary items, including eating out, entertainment and holidays.

People are frequently surprised to discover exactly how much money they spend on transitory lifestyle items. Having a coffee at Starbucks every day, for example, can easily cost you more than £600 a year. This part of the financial plan can be a useful time to evaluate how many of the things you spend money on today are ones you might be willing or able to give up in order to have more wealth and security in the future.

Estate planning

Preparing your financial plan is also a good stage to think about the future of your children and wider family when you die. If you die young or unexpectedly, life insurance can provide part of the answer. The same goes for critical illness cover. But for anyone who expects to live a normal span it is essential both to have some investments and to think through what might happen to those investments after you have gone. This in particular may require some professional help, as the difficult tax and legal consequences of death can almost invariably be ameliorated by careful advance planning.

---

3. How much you can invest

Once you have the basic income and outgoings, the next step is to try and calculate roughly how much you need to invest today, and for how long, in order to obtain the level of capital or income return that you are likely to want in the future. A number of factors are involved in this:

- future inflation rates

- potential investment returns

- taxes and costs

- your investment time frame.

It is particularly important to make realistic assumptions about your life expectancy. This applies especially to pensions, which remain most people's biggest financial asset after their home. Thanks to medical advances and improvements in standards of living, human beings now live much longer than they did. Life expectancy for the average man is now ten years longer than it was 30 years ago: for women it is 12 years longer. If you are thinking of retiring at the normal age, you are going to have to rely on your savings for much longer in order to go on enjoying the lifestyle that you have planned or hope to have.

Possible future inflation rates

Inflation is one of the most potent and insidious risks facing anyone who chooses to save and invest money. Even modest rates of inflation, like the ones we have experienced in the last few years, can quickly destroy the purchasing power of your money.

If inflation is running at 2% per annum, what you can buy with £100 will decline by 18% (almost a fifth) after ten years and by 32% (or nearly a third) after 20 years. In a normal working lifetime of 40 years, the purchasing power of your money will fall by 55%

(more than half) if inflation is 2% per annum. If it goes to 5% per annum, the value of every £100 you have today will be just £16 in 'real' terms when you quit working after 40 years.[1]

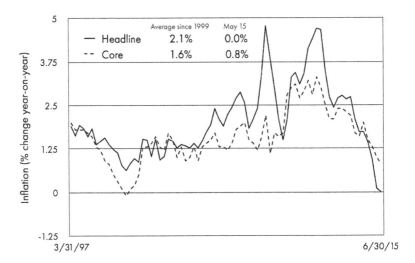

Figure 2.1: Inflation since the turn of the century – up for 10 years, then falling fast. The core consumer price index (CPI) excludes food and energy: the headline CPI includes them. What matters most to you, however, is the cost of the lifestyle you have chosen.

Source: J.P.Morgan Asset Management, Guide to the Markets.

That is generally good news, but it does not tell the whole story. Many of the essential things that you have to pay for in life, such as heating and lighting, water, insurance and food (and housing!), are still going up in price more quickly than official inflation figures suggest. A fundamental principle of good investment is that unless your investments can grow at least as fast as the cost of your lifestyle, you are not getting any wealthier – as many people found out in

---

[1]   'Real' is the word that economists use to describe what something is worth after deducting the effect of inflation.

the 1970s, when inflation soared to more than 25% and wiped out the savings of those who had not prepared for such an outcome.

Our current issues are not the same, but don't be misled into thinking that runaway inflation like that could not happen again. It can and quite probably will, though I don't know when. The point is that your investment strategy must take account of the possibility. Only if your income and investments can grow by more than the rate of inflation will you be able to afford the same things when you retire as you spend money on today.

Potential rates of return

You cannot know how much you will need to invest without also having an idea of the possible returns that you might be able to make. Putting it at its simplest, there are four main asset classes that investors have to consider. Any sensible investment strategy is likely to include a mixture of these type of investments, which all have their own distinctive characteristics. In all four cases you have the choice of investing directly yourself or using a managed investment fund to gain your exposure. The four are:

- equities (the posh word for shares)
- bonds (fixed-interest securities)
- property
- cash.

With the help of historical surveys, it is possible to summarise the historic returns that these four asset classes have produced over long periods of time. It is easy to start with cash, which means not just the money in your purse or wallet but the money you have deposited in the bank or building society. A few years ago it was possible to earn 4%–5% on your deposits, and even though inflation was higher than today it still left you ahead of the rate of inflation.

Since the global financial crisis of 2008, however, that is no longer the case. Interest rates, which are the main weapon that policymakers have to control inflation, have also fallen to record low levels as inflation has subsided. The basic lending rate set by the Bank of England was cut to just 0.5% after the crisis – its lowest level for six centuries – and was still at that rock-bottom rate five years later. That in turn has resulted in derisory returns on deposits at the bank and building society.

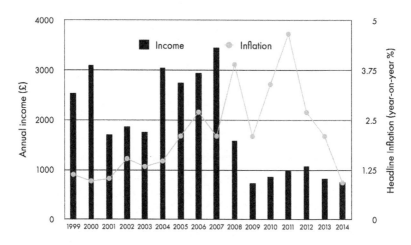

Figure 2.2: Returns on bank deposits have fallen dramatically since the global financial crisis in 2008. Having been above the rate of inflation before, they have been well below for several years – not a happy state of affairs for investors.

Source: J.P.Morgan Asset Management.

What about the other so-called 'asset classes' I mentioned above? In Table 2.1 I show the annualised rates of return achieved by the different asset classes over long periods of history. At first glance all these figures may seem pitifully small. But remember (a) that these are returns *after* allowing for inflation; and (b) that they represent the long-run annual percentage *rate* of growth for each class. The table does not bring out the effect of compounding those modest annualised returns over long periods of time. (For commercial property and index-linked gilts, we do not have such a long series of figures as we do for the others, so the historical record is shorter.)

Asset type	10 years	20 years	30 years	50 years
Equities	4.1	4.6	6.2	5.4
Conventional gilts	3.7	5.1	5.2	3.1
Commercial property	2.7	5.6	5.6	-
Residential property	-0.3	3.6	2.4	-
Index-linked gilts	3.5	4.4	3.9	-
T-bills (cash)	-0.7	1.1	2.5	1.5
Building society	-1.5	0.0	1.3	0.8
After deducting inflation	**3.1**	**2.9**	**3.5**	**5.6**

Table 2.1: The long run returns from different asset classes after inflation.
This table measures the annual percentage real return from shares, bonds, property and cash over different time periods (data as 31st December 2014). While shares typically produce the highest returns, over shorter periods they can be much more volatile. Another point to note is that bond returns have been well above their long term historical average in the last 20 years and are unlikely to be that good in the next 20 years.

You may be surprised – most first-time investors are – by the enormous positive impact that the wonders of compounding can do for your financial wellbeing. The way to see how dramatic this effect can be is to translate rates of return into cumulative monetary sums. In Table 2.2 I show the long term impact on your wealth if your investments earn a given rate of return over time. You can easily see how even small sums invested at seemingly modest rates of return can grow into something pretty big if you let time do its work. For example if you invest just £1,000 and make a 7% annual rate of return every year, after 20 years, provided you have drawn nothing out, you will have £3,870 – nearly 3.9 times as much as you put in. After 30 years your investment will have grown 7.6 times and after 40 years no less than 14.9 times.

The value of £1,000 invested

Assuming no inflation

| Growth rate | Number of years invested | | | | |
	10	20	30	40	50
3%	£1,344	£1,806	£2,427	£3,262	£4,384
5%	£1,629	£2,653	£4,322	£7,040	£11,467
7%	£1,967	£3,870	£7,612	£14,974	£29,457
10%	£2,594	£6,727	£17,449	£45,259	£117,391
Invested	£1,000	£1,000	£1,000	£1,000	£1,000

Table 2.2: The impact of compounding your money over time.
This table shows the effect of investing money at different rates of return over long periods of time. If your working life extends to 40 years, there is clearly a lot of scope to build a worthwhile investment fund or pension pot.

The wonder of compounding is that the higher the growth rate you can achieve, and the longer you are able to invest, the bigger that eventual multiple will be – and the more your investment fund will be worth. This, as I have already mentioned, is one of the most important lessons in thinking about investment: time really is money. It is the fundamental reason why those who can start investing early in life are handsomely rewarded. It is also the reason why the rich tend to get richer. Having money to start with means they have much longer to reap the rewards of investing than someone who has to work their way up to becoming an investor for the first time in say their 40s or 50s.

The figures I have shown are cash figures, before taking account of inflation. The bad news is that inflation also has a compounding effect on the purchasing power of the money you have invested. You need to factor in a future inflation rate to arrive at the final 'real' or purchasing power value of your investments. So if you assume a future inflation rate of 2.0% per annum, for example, the figures come out as in Table 2.3. You can see how the multiple of your investment – how far your wealth can grow in real terms – declines as a result.

The value of £1,000 invested

After inflation at 2% per annum

| Growth rate | Number of years invested | | | | |
	10	20	30	40	50
3%	£1,102	£1,215	£1,340	£1,477	£1,629
5%	£1,336	£1,786	£2,386	£3,188	£4,260
7%	£1,614	£2,604	£4,203	£6,782	£10,944
10%	£2,128	£4,527	£9,633	£20,497	£43,614
Invested	£1,000	£1,000	£1,000	£1,000	£1,000

Table 2.3: The impact of compounding your money over time, in real terms, after accounting for inflation of 2% per annum.

After 20 years, to take the same example as before, your fund has grown by just over two and a half times what you have put in, as opposed to nearly 3.7 times before inflation. That is still a big improvement on leaving your money uninvested, but also a useful reality check about how corrosive inflation can be. Over 40 and 50 years the difference between the pre- and post-inflation value of your notional investment fund is even wider still. Inflation at just 2% can wipe out as much as a half to two thirds of the amount you would have had if there had been no inflation.

If we now go back and look again at the table of returns from the main asset classes, you can see the importance of looking at inflation-adjusted figures rather than the raw returns. We can translate the actual returns on offer over the last few decades and translate them into what they would be worth today, given a range of different starting points. The annualised rates of return may appear very modest, but in practice, thanks to compounding, they have generated significant sums for anyone who has been able to go down the investing route.

Real value of £1,000 invested

At historical rates of return

	Number of years invested			
	10	**20**	**30**	**50**
Equities	£1,495	£2,458	£6,078	£13,869
Conventional gilts	£1,438	£2,704	£4,576	£4,602
Commercial property	£1,305	£2,951	£5,055	-
Residential property	£970	£2,068	£2,037	-
Index-linked gilts	£1,411	£2,366	£3,151	-
Cash	£932	£1,245	£2,098	£2,105
Building society	£860	£1,000	£1,473	£1,489
Historic inflation rate	3.1%	2.9%	3.5%	5.6%

Table 2.4: Long run returns in monetary terms.

It is easier to grasp what real returns mean in practice by expressing the figures in the table above as cash sums – the amount you would have had at the end of each time period, again after adjusting for inflation. The points to note are (a) that the wonder of compounding helps returns grow disproportionately large as time goes by; (b) that investing in the right assets can make a material difference to your wealth; and (c) that so-called risk assets like shares and property tend to produce the highest returns over time, although not consistently over all periods.

See your finances in the round

One of the biggest mistakes I have found people make is failing to see their finances in the round. They tend to think of their house, their pension, their investments and their cash reserves as distinct 'buckets', rather than as what they really are: just different elements of one bigger picture. The various pieces may have different tax and risk characteristics, which certainly need to be taken into account, but in reality it is the overall balance of your money that is going to determine how well you fare in achieving your objectives.

Most people want to own their own home and that typically provides them with nearly all the exposure to property they need (although buy-to-let has become a fashionable option which I discuss later[2]). The biggest question for DIY investors is mainly about how they divide up their remaining financial assets between equities, bonds and cash. Bonds and cash are typically used to provide lower but more certain returns, while equities provide the best hope, other than property, for beating inflation and achieving higher but less certain capital and income gains over the longer term.

From the tables you can also clearly see that equities and property have historically provided the highest returns, both before and more importantly after adjusting for inflation. They are sometimes called 'real assets' for this reason. These higher returns come at a price, however, which is much greater volatility. What that means is that while they typically produce the best results in the end, you have to live with the fact that their value moves

---

2   See chapter 8 for my thoughts on buy-to-let.

up and down more dramatically from one year to the next. That makes them inherently riskier, at least in the short term.

It is important also to note that the long-term averages are just that – averages. The pattern of returns from the four main asset classes can vary a lot from one period to the next. In the next table I show the annual rates of return of the big four asset classes from one ten-year period to the next, going back to the start of the 20th century (we don't have good enough data for the others going back that far). The first half of the 20th century, for example, which included two world wars, produced a very different pattern of returns to the second half, which was more peaceful but included a period of very high global inflation.

The ranking of the four asset classes can also change over time. Over the long run, equities come out on top, ahead of property, followed by bonds and cash – but there is nothing pre-ordained about that result. In any ten or 20-year period the order can be reversed, depending on the prevailing historical circumstances. What works best at one point won't work so well at another. For example, if you use the figures from 1990, they show that government bonds (also known as gilts) have produced almost exactly the same return as those of shares – something that has happened rarely in the past. (There are some specific reasons for that, mainly to do with the fact that the last 30 years have been marked by a long and steady decline in the level of interest rates, not just in the UK but in most countries around the world. Falling interest rates are generally good for fixed-interest securities like bonds, and vice versa.)

Real investment returns (% pa)				
	Equities	**Gilts**	**Index-linked**	**Cash**
1904–1914	2.1	-0.1		1.5
1914–24	0.4	-3.1		-1.7
1924–34	9.2	11.7		5.6
1934–44	3.0	-1.4		-2.4
1944–54	5.3	-2.6		-2.8
1954–64	7.1	-2.6		1.4
1964–74	-6.0	-6.3		0.0
1974–84	17.4	5.6		-0.3
1984–94	9.4	5.8	2.8	5.5
1994–2004	5.0	6.5	5.3	3.0
2004–2014	4.1	3.7	3.5	-0.7

Table 2.5. Real investment returns by decade.
Every decade in history produces a different pattern of returns by asset class. But there has only been one decade since the start of the 20th century when equities produced negative returns, and several when gilts and cash did so – in every case as the result of inflation eroding the real value of investors' savings. The trouble is that while equities produce the best long-term returns, they have fallen more than once by as much as 50% over shorter periods than a decade, which scares many people out of sticking with them. The first index-linked gilt was issued in 1981 so there is no earlier history.

Source: Barclays Research

The final point to make here is that a lot depends on when you start investing and whether the asset classes you buy are relatively cheap or expensive at the time you buy them. The cheaper they are, the better they are likely to perform over time – that is common sense. If they are expensive, the odds are you won't do as well as the historical averages. While there is no guarantee that future rates of return will be similar to those achieved in the past, the historical pattern is sufficiently consistent to make it reasonable to use the averages as a general starting point for looking to what might happen in the future. Learning to assess whether the price of financial assets are a bargain or a steal is an important part of the investor's challenge. If you can invest regularly – so much a month – the valuation issue is not quite so important, as things tend to even out over time.

The importance of avoiding taxes

The figures I have quoted take no account of tax. It is obvious that the more tax you can avoid paying as your investments grow, the bigger the amount you will have left at the end of the process. Back in the 1970s it was difficult to avoid paying tax on investment gains. Today that is no longer the case, thanks to those powerful tax incentives which I mentioned in chapter 1 (see 'ISAs, SIPPs and pensions' on the next page). An important reason why it so essential to make maximum use of the tax allowances and other exemptions that the government makes available is that any money you can save and avoid paying tax on can also benefit from the wonders of compounding.

Think of it like this. Every £1,000 you can save legitimately from the grasp of the taxman each year is freed to go on growing for the rest of your life if you invest it – becoming, potentially, a huge and tidy sum. If you can save an extra £1,000 a year by avoiding tax for the next 40 years, assuming that money can be invested to make a return of 5% a year, the extra you have saved and invested will be worth no less than £134,000 at the end of that period. Put it another way: if you are lucky enough to be able to save £8,000 a year from the taxman, it could be worth more than £1 million by the time you retire 40 years later.

ISAs, SIPPs and pensions

The first thing any investor should do is check out the tax breaks which the government offers to those who save and invest. There are different advantages to saving into an Individual Savings Account (an ISA) and saving for a pension. In my view, most people should aim to do both as soon as they can. The chancellor also announced in 2015 that the first £5,000 of dividend income from shares and the first £1,000 of interest on bank and building society deposits, even if held outside an ISA 'tax wrapper', can also be received free of income tax.

The attraction of ISAs is that any gains and income you receive from the investments you hold within this tax wrapper will remain exempt from tax, whatever the amounts involved, and however long you hold them. The annual limit on the amount you can pay each year into an ISA is now more than £15,000 and the limits are normally increased each year, meaning that for most people all their investing can effectively be done tax-free. Funds, shares and cash are all capable of being held inside an ISA. Any money held in an ISA does not have to be included in your annual tax return.

The tax savings on pension contributions can potentially be even greater, as the basic principle is that any contributions you make to your pension scheme (whether it is a personal pension or a company scheme) qualify for tax relief up to certain annual and lifetime limits. As of 2015, if you are a higher-rate taxpayer that means every £100 you put aside for your pension effectively reduces your income tax bill by 40% of that amount. For standard-rate taxpayers, the rate is 20%.

Self-invested personal pensions, known as SIPPs, have become popular vehicles for many investors, although the government continues – annoyingly – to change the rules on how much tax relief you can receive from one year to the next. In 2015, except for the highest earners, who are more harshly treated, the maximum annual contribution you could claim tax relief for was set at £40,000 a year. There was also a lifetime limit of £1m. (The annual limits are a relatively new thing, and there may be scope to add more money by using up prior year allowances that have been not used.)

The great advantage of an ISA is that you can take the capital out at any time without having to pay any further tax, whereas with any kind of pension, under the current rules, you can only take out a maximum of 25% of your accumulated savings as tax-free cash after the age of 55. Any additional withdrawals, however you take them, are taxable at your marginal tax rate. Under the latest government rules, you are no longer required to buy an annuity at the age of 75, as was the case before.

Confused? Understanding what is going on in the pensions field is frankly a bit of a nightmare, as the rules change almost every year (and will do again in 2016). It is one area where specialist advice is definitely worth taking. The good news is that there is plenty of information about the pension rules online – both on official government sites and elsewhere.

A good investment platform will summarise the latest rules for you and my advice is that you should check what they are at least once a year. The key point is that investing in a pension, as with an ISA, is a highly tax-efficient way to invest and one of the obvious options for any would-be DIY investor to consider.

Don't forget costs

As well as taxes, the figures I have quoted about asset-class returns also exclude the cost of investing. Any kind of investment inevitably carries costs with it. The higher the cost, the better the investment has to do in order to justify what you have paid for it. Unfortunately, the real cost of investing is often much higher than it may appear, as we'll cover later in this book. It is vitally important to understand exactly what costs you are incurring. Only then can you know if they are worth it or whether they are going to eat too far into the returns you can make as an investor.

It makes a huge difference whether an investment that earns 5% a year costs 1% or 2% per annum to own. The good news is that the costs of investing are starting to come down and DIY investing has become more cost-effective than in the past.

Putting it all together

To summarise, how much money your investments will make over time depends on the investment returns you can obtain *after* the deduction of tax and costs. What you can then do with that money will be determined by how successful you are in beating inflation. Your objective is to maximise the 'real' return on your investments after taking account of taxes, costs and one other crucial factor – risk. Different types of investment carry different levels of risk. Shares, for example, are generally riskier than fixed-income investments. A riskier investment is one that may produce a higher rate of return, but only at the cost of a higher chance of loss.

The only certain way to reduce your risk is to diversify: to spread your investments across a range of different investments. Not all types of investment move in tandem, so a well-balanced portfolio will not rise and fall as dramatically as one that has all its eggs in one basket – say, 100% in shares or property. In general, you have a better chance of obtaining a higher rate of return from a risky investment the longer you are able to hold it. It follows that the more years of investing you have ahead of you, the greater the chance of doing exceptionally – rather than averagely – well. It also follows that the earlier in life you can start investing for the future, the better off you stand to become.

Whatever you are investing for, the minimum length of time you should think about when planning an investment programme, I suggest, is five years – ideally even longer. Good investing is like an ideal marriage: you hope that it will last the whole of your life. Sometimes you may be pleasantly surprised to reach your target ahead of time, but don't count on it. If you really do need the money on a shorter time horizon, you should consider more certain homes for your money, such as cash or fixed interest, even though the returns will almost certainly be much lower. You should only ever think about investing capital in riskier asset classes knowing that in the short term it could decline in value.

Equity performance						
	Number of consecutive years					
	2	**3**	**4**	**5**	**10**	**18**
Outperform cash	77	79	81	83	96	97
Underperform cash	37	43	31	28	10	1
Total number of years	114	113	112	111	106	98
Probability of equity outperformance	68%	70%	72%	75%	91%	99%
Outperform gilts	78	84	84	81	84	85
Underperform gilts	36	29	28	30	22	13
Total number of years	114	113	112	111	106	98
Probability of equity outperformance	68%	74%	75%	73%	79%	87%

Table 2.6: The odds on equities outperforming gilts and cash.
As long as history repeats itself, the longer you own a portfolio of shares, the more likely it is that they will do better than safer alternatives such as cash or gilts. Over five years, in both cases the chances that you will do better from equities is around 75% on this basis.

The good news for any investor who starts early is that the longer you can invest the better you are likely to do – and the more certain your returns are going to be. As the next chart illustrates, the range of returns from different asset classes narrows with the passage of time: the good and bad years tend to cancel each other out. In the same way the likelihood that riskier assets such as equities and property will outperform increases the longer you are able to hold them. Historically, if you are able to own equities for more than 20 years, the odds are over 90% that you will do better than keeping your money in cash.

Maximum and minimum real returns over various periods

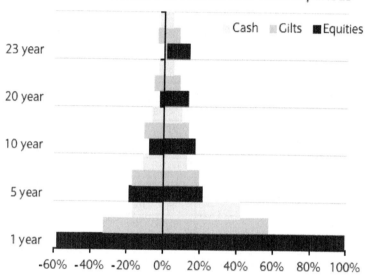

Figure 2.3: How the passage of time reduces the variability of asset class returns.

Source: Barclays Equity Gilt Study 2015.

Projecting future returns is never easy and it is only fair to say that it is particularly hazardous today. The years since the financial crisis in 2008 have been characterised by very different conditions to earlier historical periods. With interest rates at such unprecedentedly low levels, no period in my lifetime has been quite like it. Policymakers have set out to make it easier for everyone – governments, businesses and individuals – to cope with the aftermath of the crisis, which has left the world lumbered with massive and unprecedented amounts of debt.

On the plus side, the low-interest policy has slashed the cost of mortgages and provided short-term relief for many of those struggling to repay what they owe. The downside is that the policy has also heavily distorted the traditional ways of valuing financial assets – working out, in other words, whether shares and bonds are cheap, expensive or about fair value. In practice the policy has had the effect of driving up the price of many financial assets to what seem very high levels by historical standards. However, you can be sure that it is not going to stay that way for ever.

The bottom line

Taking all these factors into account should allow you to come up with a figure for the kind of financial contribution or regular investment you are likely to need, and an idea of how long you will have to make it, in order to have a reasonable chance of meeting your financial targets in the future. I go on in the rest of the book to explain how to use investment funds to achieve the kind of objective that you might set yourself having done such an exercise.

Here is a simple example. Suppose you invest £5,000 a year for 30 years – how much will you have at the end? I have worked out some illustrative figures, based on the following assumptions.

The investor has no tax to pay, thanks to using an ISA. The money is invested 65% in the stock market, 25% in different types of bonds, 10% in property and 5% in cash. Inflation averages 2%. Real rates of return assumed are equities 5%, bonds 2%, property 5% and cash 1%. The investor, as I do, uses funds to obtain the property and equity weightings. I have deducted representative fees from those funds. This produces overall rate of return of 5.6% per annum before and 3.6% after inflation.

Remember that this is a theoretical exercise. There is no guarantee that the results will be as I have said.[3] If my assumptions turn out to be valid, however, you will have around £385,000 at the end of the period, having invested £150,000 along the way. After 40 years, with the full effect of long-run compounding coming through, your investment pot will nearly have doubled again, to approximately £725,000 in value.

There are two ways in which you might react to these figures. One is to say, "Gosh, those final numbers are surprisingly large, even for what seem like very small rates of return." The other is to say: "Oh dear, even if I am lucky and get a reasonably high rate of return, I am still not going to end up with enough for my future needs." In reality both responses are perfectly valid. On the one hand it is rare that I meet anyone who has done this kind of planning exercise who comes away thinking, "I am investing too much." Most people, I know from experience, should be doing a lot more than they are. On the other hand I also rarely

---

3   Because this is a long-run planning exercise, I am assuming that returns will at some stage revert to their long-run historical averages. The money invested today, as opposed to in future years, may produce lower returns, given relatively high valuations at the time of writing.

come across anyone who isn't heartened and encouraged by the remarkable way in which even little sums, saved regularly, can compound over time into something much bigger.

You can see again from this example how the value of the investments starts to grow faster as the number of years goes up – that is compounding again. By the end of the 30-year period, the value of your investments will be 2.57 times the amount you have put in. Of course in the real world, the progress won't be as smooth as this. There will be lots of ups and downs along the way. But note also this: if you could improve the annual rate of return by just 2% per annum, the final sum would not be 2.57, but 3.53 times as great as the total amount you put aside – an extra £175,000 in round figures! Small differences in investment returns can make for hugely different outcomes if you let time do its work. It is all the more reason to get started straightaway, however small the amount you can afford – and all the more reason to put an effort into finding the best extra unit of return.

Lump sums or regular contributions?

Is it better to invest a lump sum or make regular contributions to your investment pot? My answer is: it does not necessarily matter. In real life most of us combine periods when we are able to save regularly with others when we are unable to afford anything at all. Once every few years you may find yourself with a one-off lump sum to invest – from a legacy perhaps, or redundancy, or the payoff from some shares or share options. My advice to clients tends to be: try to save what you can afford on a regular basis, but be willing and happy to top it up with a bigger sum if and when a cash windfall comes along. Think of regular investing as good discipline and one-off sums as a welcome bonus.

Sensible to start simply

In the old days, when I met a person with a lump sum, in order to give them some guidance I would normally start by saying something like: "Why not split the lump sum into thirds – one third cash, one third fixed-interest and one third equities?" I still think that is a good starting point for newcomers to investing; it is easy to remember and there is logic behind it. It recognises that the important thing for any investor is to become comfortable with what they are trying to do. As you go on and get more experienced, and as your circumstances change, you can start to think of changing the percentages and giving more thought to how you split up the three components (What kind of equities? What kind of bonds? And so on), as I did in the example above.

Is having a third of your money in cash a good idea as a starting point? Between 2000 and 2008 the answer was clearly yes – interest rates on cash were much higher then (and we all stupidly thought that banks knew what they were doing and money deposited with them was safe!). It is harder to justify today when interest rates are so low, but you always need to compare the return, as I have said, with both your actual cost of living and your appetite for risk. If the prices of the things you need or want are falling, even cash that earns no interest can still leave you better off at the end of the year and you have not risked losing anything in the process.

To take another example, if you've just retired or are coming up to retirement, you also might want to start off with at least 50% in cash. Why? Because you can't be quite sure how things will go in your first couple of years of retirement. People often find that what they actually spend is different to what they expected. You should not be in a rush to tie all your money up straight away. It is always a good idea to stop and think what you're trying to do. Look at all the options and take your time. You won't regret it. It is a big decision you are making.

For those who are starting out, or investing on a regular basis while still quite young, the issues are not so difficult. The younger you are, and the longer you have to see your investments bear fruit, the more logical it is to put more of your money into riskier equities and property. If you can afford to wait for the good years to cancel out the bad, and are investing on a regular basis, it matters much less whether what you are buying appears cheap or expensive. As the years go by, the price you pay for what you own will average out, and the returns you get will move closer to the long-run historical averages. The weightings that I used in the long-term portfolio example above (60% in equities, 25% in bonds, 10% in property and 5% in cash) might be more appropriate.

Once you have been through the planning exercise, the next challenge is how to make the investments that will give you the best chance of meeting the objectives you have worked out in your financial plan. This is where funds and investment platforms come into their own.

Points to remember

- The primary objective of investment is to improve your quality of life.

- Money spent on a financial plan is almost always money well-spent.

- If you do nothing with your money, you cannot end up with any more than you started with.

- Asset-allocation means deciding how to allocate your money between equities, bonds, property and cash.

- Wealth only grows if you can outpace inflation in the things you want or need.

- Shares and property have provided the highest returns historically, but bonds have done equally well since 1990.

- Small increases in rates of return can be extremely valuable if you let time do its work.

- Whatever else you do, make sure you take advantage of tax breaks on ISAs and pension contributions.

CHAPTER 3.
Getting Started

S O YOU HAVE DECIDED TO START MAKING REGULAR SAVINGS into an investment programme. Maybe you are already an investor but want to rethink whether you are approaching it the best way. Or maybe you have just come into a lump sum. The same questions always then arise: how do I go about investing? And what is the best way to put those investment decisions into practice? In this chapter I give my views on these questions. I explain why for most people I believe the answer to, "Why use funds?" is: "Because it is the simplest and most convenient way to do it", and the answer to, "How?" is: "By using an investment platform".

Of course, you may say that, working for one of the largest platform providers in the country and specialising in fund research, I am simply 'talking my book' – well, yes, but please hear me out. There is a reason so many more investors invest in funds than directly in stocks and shares. And there is a reason why the use of investment platforms is growing so rapidly every year and such platforms now account for 50% of all fund business.

Whether you are buying funds, shares or both (as many do), they are the simplest and most convenient solutions investors can choose. In making my case, I am only echoing the way that investors themselves have voted with their wallets and the way that most sensible professionals do it too.

Why invest in funds?

I have been researching and analysing investment funds all my working life. They have been my professional speciality for as long as I care to remember. My own money is predominantly invested in funds rather than in individual stocks and shares. Even without knowing your personal circumstances, I am confident that funds are probably the way you should be investing too.[4] Funds are the building blocks from which you are going to construct your overall investment portfolio. Pick them sensibly and you are on course to do well: but pick them randomly, or without the right guidance, and you run the risk of disappointment.

A one-minute history

Investment funds have been around for a long time in one form or another. First there were investment trusts, which date originally from the 19th century, and some of which, like the venerable Foreign & Colonial Investment Trust, are still with us. Then in the 1930s came the first unit trusts (or mutual funds, as

---

4   I cannot know that for certain. To be sure I would need to know your personal circumstances, your relevant knowledge and experience, and your tolerance for risk. However, the generalisation remains valid.

the Americans know them). The honour of being the first unit trust in the UK goes to M&G, a company that is still going strong today. It created the first UK unit trust in 1931.

Unit trusts started to become popular consumer items in the 1960s and have continued to grow steadily in popularity ever since then, punctuated by periods of innovation and change. The most notable recent innovations came in the 1990s with the launch of the first open-ended investment company (OEIC) and the first exchange-traded fund, or ETF for short. Other variants, such as horribly named UCITS 3 funds, have also come on the scene.

Frankly, whoever came up with these stupid names and abbreviations deserves to be shot, as all these different and strangely named creatures are basically variants of the same thing. For simplicity and convenience, like most people in the business, I prefer to give them all the umbrella name of 'investment funds'. And that is because the basic idea behind all of the types I have mentioned is the same.

What funds offer you as an investor is the opportunity to pool your money with that of hundreds or thousands of other investors in a single entity which is managed or administered on your behalf by a professional investment manager. The legal structure differs from one type of fund to another, as does the kind of things that they invest in, but what they all have in common is that each investor holds units, or shares, in the fund and each unit has the same value as any other.

That makes funds, among other things, a very democratic way of putting your money to work. But there are other more important reasons why funds have become so popular over the years. They can be summed up as: convenience, diversification and tax. As I explain in chapter 7, the great majority of my own money is invested in funds for these very reasons.

There are some disadvantages, which I shall come to, but it is important to start with the advantages, as the worst thing you can do in investment is be talked out of a good thing for the wrong reason. Let me therefore quickly expand on the fundamental strengths of funds as I see them. For the purpose of this exercise the funds I am referring to are usually unit trusts and OEICs, which are broadly similar (see the separate box for how they differ). I discuss later why I generally – but by no means exclusively – prefer these kinds of funds to investment trusts, exchange-traded funds (known as ETFs) and other variants. I also explain why I do, however, make use of one kind of investment trust, known as a venture capital trust (or VCT), for my own portfolio.

Fund types

Unit trusts and OEICs (open-ended investment companies) are two variants of what are called open-ended funds. When investors buy units, or shares, in a fund like this they become entitled to their share of any gains or income the fund generates. The size of the fund rises and falls in response to investor demand. When demand exceeds supply, the fund management company issues new units, and when sellers outnumber buyers, it cancels ('redeems') them instead.

While their legal and corporate governance structure is somewhat different, for practical purposes the only real difference between the

---

two types of open-ended fund is that with an OEIC, the buying and selling price is the same, while for unit trusts there is a 'spread' between the two (made up of the bid and offer price respectively.) The price of open-ended funds is determined by the value of the investments that the fund makes, after the management charges have been deducted.

Investment trusts, also known as closed-ended funds, differ from unit trusts and OEICs in having a fixed capital structure rather than one which ebbs and flows with supply and demand. Investors own shares in the trust and unlike open-ended funds, these can be bought and sold on the stock market. There is, however, no guarantee that the share price will always be the same as the value of the investments which the trust owns – another difference from unit trusts and OEICs. (See chapter 8 for more of my thoughts about investment trusts.) Exchange-traded funds amalgamate some features of both open-ended and closed-ended funds. It is easiest to think of them as unit trusts that can be traded on the stock market like any other share. As such they are more likely to be used for short-term trading than for long-term investment.

Convenience

The first fundamental reason for investing in funds is they take most of the hassle out of what can otherwise be a time-consuming and frustrating exercise. By investing in funds you are effectively delegating most of the heavy lifting to someone else. A fund in that respect is quite a lot like a syndicate, where you pool your money with others to buy a racehorse or do the lottery. As part owner of a racehorse, you get to go to the course on race days, pose for photos and (very occasionally) collect some winnings, but you are not the one who has to get up at 5 o'clock in the morning to gallop your horse in the freezing cold and call in the vet when it catches a chill.

So it is with a fund: the professional fund manager makes the buy and sell decisions for all the investors in the fund and you get to enjoy the fruits of any success without having to do any of the hard work. (Before you get the wrong idea, I should emphasise that the rewards from investing are much greater and a whole lot more reliable than those you get from owning a racehorse or doing the lottery.) With the advent of sophisticated IT systems, these days you don't even have to fill out and sign a form to buy or sell units in an investment fund. You can do it all with a couple of clicks of the mouse. Someone else takes care of all the paperwork and admin too.

Scale and diversification

A second crucial benefit of investing in a fund is that pooling your money with others has a number of practical advantages when it comes to making investment decisions. For a start it greatly widens the choice of investments you can make, allowing you to make investments all over the world, not just in the UK. This is true whether your main area of interest is buying shares in a company (equity investment) or investing in bonds (fixed-income investing). Professional fund managers also have access to much more information and research than any individual investor can obtain.[5]

The largest fund management firms have specialists in almost every kind of investment you may wish to make. They also have years of experience in making investment decisions. These days

---

[5]   As I said earlier, the amount of information private investors now have access to is as good as most professionals had 20 years ago, but professionals still have the edge.

they even have to be qualified to do so – not something that was always the case in the past! Once upon a time they were also able to trade stocks and shares more cheaply than you, although this advantage has diminished with the advent of low-cost dealing services for private investors. (These days, by shopping around, you can buy and sell shares through a platform for as little as £7.50 a trade.)

Investing in a fund is also the simplest way to obtain the benefits of diversification, which is every investor's best protection against the risk of loss and personal stupidity. In order to be able to take money from investors, funds are required to spread their investments across a minimum number of instruments. By pooling investors' money, and then spreading that pool of money across a wide range of individual stocks and shares, a typical fund provides an important degree of diversification that individual investors could not achieve without doing a lot more work themselves. Fund investors only have to make one decision, to buy and sell a fund. All the other decisions are delegated.

Tax benefits

A third key feature of funds stems directly from the fact that they are managed by professional investment managers, acting on your behalf. As investing money for others is their sole business, HM Revenue & Customs gives funds an exemption from paying tax on the investments they buy and sell, so long as that money remains within the fund. It means that any money you keep invested in a fund can go on compounding in value without the taxman dipping in every year to take a chunk of it away. Because of the wonders of compounding, this can have a material effect on how big your investment pot will grow to become over time.

The advantage of funds in this respect has diminished somewhat in recent years thanks to the generous tax concessions that successive governments have introduced for individual investors, which I described in the last chapter. Because only a small number of people earn enough to be able to invest more than their £15,240 a year ISA allowance, in practice this means that investing tax-free has become a feasible option for the majority of investors. Investment funds also make excellent building blocks for a pension, as you can take advantage of the generous tax relief on contributions, even if the amount you can invest each year without paying tax has been much reduced in recent years.[6] Most company schemes now offer you the option to pick your own funds from a menu of alternatives. The convenience and diversification benefits of funds are just as valuable in this context as they are for more general investment. Despite what you might read in the press, the costs of investing through a pension fund have fallen quite sharply in recent years.

Problems with fund investing

If these are the primary advantages of investing in funds, what are the drawbacks or challenges of using funds? I would single out three in particular.

---

6   There is no guarantee that these reliefs will still be available in the same form in future, as the rules and limits are changed by the chancellor almost every year.

The first is a result of how successful the fund industry has become. Because funds are so simple and convenient to invest in, they have become very big business. Annual sales of unit trusts and OEICs have averaged around £15 billion a year over the last ten years. The amount invested in them at the end of 2014 reached £800 billion. Selling and managing funds is a profitable and competitive business and as a result the number of funds on offer to investors has grown like Topsy.

Today there are more than 3,000 authorised unit trusts and OEICs to choose from and at least 100 companies that sell them. The range and type of things they invest in also covers a wide spectrum. The choice, in other words, has become overwhelming. While the best funds are very good, the majority – 90% of them, to be brutally honest – are poor value. Picking the right fund is therefore absolutely crucial.

The second issue reflects the fact that, like most good things, funds don't come free. By using your ISA allowance, and claiming tax relief on pension contributions, it is relatively easy to minimise your current tax bill. But funds themselves come with costs attached. The manager of any fund you invest in will charge each investor in the fund an **annual fee** for doing all that heavy lifting I referred to earlier. In addition, the investor often has to pay a number of additional costs that the fund manager incurs in running the fund. If you invest through a platform, the platform will also charge you a fee for looking after your money.

All these costs add up and come straight out of any return that you might make. The issue of whether funds cost and charge too much has become a big area of concern for both the industry regulator and the media in the last few years. In 2013, after years of dithering, the regulators finally banned advisors from being paid commission on fund sales. The hope was that this would increase competition and benefit consumers by making fund costs and charges more transparent and therefore help to nudge those costs lower. It hasn't quite worked out like that, although I do think that costs are set to come down (see chapter 8 for further thoughts on this important topic).

The third problem is one that applies to unit trusts and OEICs, but not to investment trusts. It has to do with the way that open-ended funds work. Being open-ended, the size of the fund fluctuates in response to supply and demand. When demand exceeds supply, funds issue more units to accommodate the new demand. Similarly, if there are more sellers than buyers, the fund cancels or redeems surplus units in the fund. That all sounds fine, and works well most of the time. It means that funds can grow quite rapidly. From time to time, however, these flows of money can have a detrimental effect on how well the fund performs.

How so? Consider the case of a fund that has done particularly well for a number of years. As more investors become aware of how well it has done, more money is pushed in its direction. But suppose by the time the money arrives in the fund, the manager has come to the conclusion that the type of investments he or she is paid to make are no longer as attractively valued as they were. The money still has to be invested that way, because that is what the fund has promised to do, but the potential returns are now much lower. Demand has turned the fund manager into a forced buyer – never a comfortable place to be.

In this case, being successful has the paradoxical effect of damaging the interests of the investors in the fund. Something similar can happen when a fund has done poorly for reasons that may also be outside the manager's control. The outflows from disgruntled investors can force the manager to sell holdings just as they are about to go up. This kind of experience is far from uncommon.[7] It underlines the need to exercise care when deciding when and how much you want to invest in funds.

A body of recent academic research tells us that the human brain, wonderfully powerful as it is, is not particularly well-attuned to making good investment decisions. Most of us suffer from unconscious and conscious biases that can work against us doing the right thing. One such bias is chasing past performance – picking funds purely on the basis that they have done well recently. Such mistakes can be costly and unfortunately there are a number of traps and pitfalls that lie in wait for the unwary fund investor which the open-ended structure tends to exacerbate.

These three issues – choice, costs and traps for the unwary – are the ones where I think most self-directed investors need to direct their efforts. I hope to be able to provide you with help on all three. The point is that while funds are a wonderfully easy and convenient instrument through which to invest, they do not absolve you from the need to take an active interest in how and what you buy. The important thing is to devote such time as you can give to your portfolio to the things that are really going to

---

7   It is true that some funds choose to restrict inflows from new investors when the management company decides it has become too big to continue their investment strategy successfully. That is normally a positive sign, as it means they are putting your interests above their own short-term profitability.

make a difference. These are not always the ones that might at first appear to be the most important.

The case for platforms

The arrival of platforms has been a great breakthrough for the DIY investor. In the same way that the motor car helped to give millions of people the ability to go where they wanted when they wanted, so investment platforms liberate everyone to access nearly all the investment opportunities which they are likely to need at their own convenience.

What is a platform? Essentially it is a one-stop website which enables you to research, buy and sell, and then manage investments, all in your own time. General Omar Bradley, of US Army fame, said about military leadership: "…amateurs talk tactics, professionals talk logistics". A platform is the logistical tool that puts you in charge of your own money in a way that was not possible before.

Most people already know how valuable the internet can be for finding out information. An investment platform gives you access to bundles of it. It is no exaggeration to say that the average individual investor can get more detailed information from websites today than any leading professional investor had at his or her fingertips 20 years ago. To have so much choice at your fingertips – and then to act on things so easily once you have decided on a course of action – is hugely valuable.

Take a look round one of the leading platforms and you will quickly see how much useful material there is to be found there.

It is a very competitive field and the range and calibre of content is improving all the time. At minimum you can expect to find details of hundreds of shares and factsheets about nearly every type of investment fund (unit trusts and OEICs, investment trusts, tracker funds and venture capital trusts). Charting functions allow you to monitor the performance of any or all of these over a period of days, months or years. By becoming a client of the host firm, you can set up an ISA, a SIPP and buy and sell both shares and funds with a few simple strokes on your computer keyboard. Dealing charges vary from platform to platform, but this is also a competitive area which helps to keep trading and other costs down. Most funds also offer commentary on recent developments in the markets.

But there is another benefit of using a good platform which is not mentioned so often, and you could argue is even more important. That is the cost-effectiveness of having someone else to do all the boring paperwork and admin for you. What you are getting with a platform is in effect your own personal 'back office'. Twenty years ago, if you bought a fund you had to do all the paperwork yourself. You would have to rely on the fund company sending you at least two valuations a year through the post. You might think, "Oh well, that's no big deal". But then, if you had 20 funds, you would have got 40 pieces of paper through the post, none of it standardised, with each one showing the key information in a different and possibly confusing way.

That made it difficult to see exactly where all your money was being invested, let alone how well you were doing overall. In practice what you really want to know is: how much did I invest?

How much income did I get? And what is it worth now? You used to have a lot of trouble trying to find that out. Now with a good platform, someone else is doing all those calculations for you, and saving the results in your personal online account. They will send you a six-monthly statement summarising everything that you have bought or sold, plus the income paid out and the current values of your holdings.

You can also, if you wish, log in every hour of the day to check how well your money is doing (not that I recommend you do any such thing). That tedious chore is partly what you are paying for. If you are only investing small amounts, like £25 a month, it may still be slightly cheaper to buy your funds directly from a fund provider. But as you progress, and the amount you have invested grows, you will quickly find that it becomes more messy and time-consuming to go on operating in the old-fashioned way.

In addition to the logistics, while it is fairly easy to do nothing if your investments are going well, as and when the markets start to do badly, or you have an admin problem, the ability to have someone to ring up for help in sorting out the problem is really important. With the best platforms, you should be able to get through to someone who knows that they are talking about within at most a minute. Filling in your tax return can be a nightmare at the best of times, but a good platform will also help fix that problem for you too, sending you a single consolidated tax certificate every year that includes all the information you need to give the taxman in one single document.

The same goes with sorting out probate after someone dies. It is so much easier for the executors and the beneficiaries to sort out all the details if you can get a single probate paper from the platform. If the person who has died has 40 different investments, as many people do, each one of them will otherwise require a separate death certificate and a probate form to process. With a platform, you only have to produce a death certificate once. There is no need to spend hours going through drawers full of paper looking for the bits of paper which you need and chucking out the ones that you don't.

Now that the new 'pension freedom' regime is in force, if you are in or approaching retirement it is worth thinking through how best to keep track of your pension savings. If you can access money directly from your SIPP as and when you want it, which is what the new regime means for many retired people, it will be more important than ever to keep track of how much you have drawn out and the tax liability that may go with that. I expect it won't be long before your platform will give you all the information you need to monitor your pensions and track the cash flow and tax information on a monthly basis.

Finally, on the investment side, it is worth recalling how much more convenient it is to have personal access to your portfolio at all times via your computer. In the old days one reason investors paid hefty fees to discretionary fund managers was the knowledge that someone would be 'looking after' their investments while they were away on business or on holiday. Now, as long as you have a mobile phone or access to a computer, you can monitor your portfolio and buy and sell investments wherever you are at any time of night or day.

Points to remember

- Investment funds pool your money with that of other investors.

- They are the simplest and most convenient way for most people to invest.

- Always look to make use of all your available tax allowances and exemptions.

- You only need a handful of funds to meet all your investment requirements.

- Costs and charges are important factors to take into account.

- There are a number of traps for the unwary first-time investor.

- A good platform will do most of your admin for you and save a lot of time and hassle.

CHAPTER 4.

Narrowing the Field

S O YOU HAVE COMPLETED YOUR FINANCIAL PLAN AND decided to begin your new investment programme. Let's say you are planning on putting aside £1,000 a month for the next ten years. You have set up an ISA to allow you to do it without having to pay any tax on the income and capital gains. Having considered all the pros and cons, you have decided, like me, that you are going to use funds rather than invest directly in individual equities and bonds, or in more complex alternatives such as investment trusts. Great! Now it is time to turn your attention to which funds are going to best suit your purpose. This is where you will immediately run into the first of the major challenges that any self-directed investor faces. It is not going to take you more than 20 minutes of research to discover for yourself what most investors soon find out for themselves – that the choice of potential investment funds out there is simply bewilderingly large.

Deconstructing the universe

If we look at UK-registered funds alone, there are 3,000 funds you can choose to buy. Globally at the last count there were 90,000! Yet a well-balanced portfolio rarely needs more than ten or 15 funds in it. This universe therefore needs some serious pruning. One of the curious statistics about the UK fund industry is that there are more UK funds investing in listed company shares than there are listed company shares for them to invest in! That is before you consider what are called offshore funds, those registered in other countries and domiciles. What is more, each fund is likely to have more than one different class of unit or share to invest in.

At this point some people either have a tendency to give up or simply plump for any name that they recognise. High street banks, for example, have always put their name to a range of funds for this very reason. They don't actually manage the funds themselves, but outsource that task to a specialist investment management firm, keeping a share of the profits on the sale for themselves. Some of the big retailers, such as Marks & Spencer and Tesco, also offer funds to their customers in the same way. There are also (inevitably, you might think) Virgin funds as well. Richard Branson was one of the first to try and muscle in on the growing demand for funds back in the 1990s, when with great fanfare he launched his own fund, which in practice, like most of his branded ventures, was managed by another company.

Unfortunately there is no guarantee that a branded fund will offer good value. Brand recognition in an unrelated field is not itself a recipe for investment success. Good funds are best found through independent research. The idea that investors would value independent help in choosing which funds to own was exactly the reason that Peter Hargreaves and Stephen Lansdown first set up their business 33 years ago. It was also, as I have mentioned, how I started out in the business myself with Kean Seagar at Whitechurch Securities. We all quickly found out how popular trying to help people through the minefield of choosing funds could be. If choosing the best funds was an easy task, firms like HL and many others would not exist.

Nevertheless there is no reason why investors should not be able to do a good deal of the homework themselves – and good reasons why, even if you end up going along with a firm's recommendations, or are merely trying to see what your financial advisor or wealth manager is doing with your money, making the effort to understand what makes the difference between a good and a bad fund will greatly improve your chances of success.

First steps

The first step in narrowing down your choices is to get a feeling for the different categories of funds available to investors. The fund industry's trade association, the Investment Association, categorises funds in two main ways: by the type of investments they make and by their investment objective. The main categories are set out in the next figure. Most of them are largely self-explanatory, although the differences between some of the equity classifications take a bit more digging into.

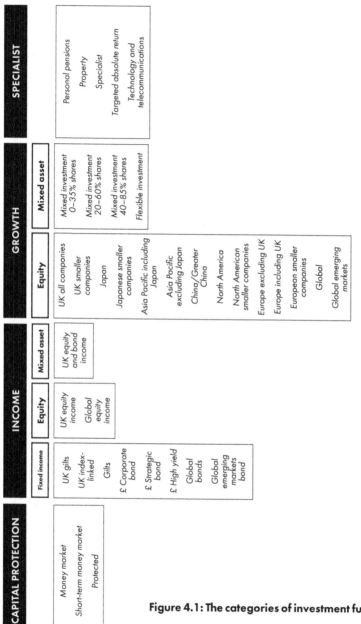

Figure 4.1: The categories of investment funds.

Source: The Investment Association.

The first cut, shown in the top line of the chart, is determined by the primary objective of the fund: is it to generate income, capital growth or some other objective? Growth and income are pretty straightforward. Capital protection refers, broadly, to cash or cash equivalents. The specialist category includes funds that invest solely in property, technology and telecommunications. Only a relatively small number of funds fall into those categories.

The next level of classification describes whether, within these categories, a fund invests primarily in equities (shares), fixed income (bonds), or some combination of these asset classes (mixed assets). Funds are also classified by whether they invest primarily in UK-listed shares and bonds or in overseas markets. Each of these categories can then be further broken down into more specific types, e.g. funds that invest solely in one country (say India) and those that invest in regions (e.g. North America or emerging markets). The fixed-income sector also has a number of different categories, depending on the kind of bond that the funds mainly invest in.[8]

If you go to the Investment Association website you can also find out how many funds there are in each category and how much money is invested in each one. For example, you will discover that around 54% of the money invested in funds goes to pure equity funds, while fixed income accounts for 15% of the total and mixed-asset funds, which combine equities, bonds and

---

8   The main types of bonds are those issued by governments (known in the UK as gilts) and those issued by companies (corporate bonds). Index-linked bonds are a special type of bond whose income and capital values are linked to the price of inflation. Corporate bonds are classified as either investment-grade, if their credit standing is good, or high-yield ('junk') if riskier.

property, another 12%. The remaining funds are property, cash and specialist funds.

Within the equity-only category, just under half of investors' money is invested in funds for whom UK stocks are their predominant focus. Global equity funds account for a further 21% while the remainder cover specific regions or countries. In fixed income the great majority of funds invest only in sterling-denominated bonds of one kind or another – with corporate bonds (issued by companies) and gilts (bonds issued by the UK government) the two largest segments.

This is the universe from which your initial choice of fund will be made. It is probably worth your while taking a few minutes to look through the definitions on the Investment Association for each category. You will pretty quickly get a reasonable picture of what is available. If the bad news about funds is that there are too many to choose from, the good news is that you can be sure that somewhere in there will be one or more funds that are ideally suited for your purpose. My job is to help you find them.

Active and passive

Two important distinctions need to be made at this point. The first is between 'actively managed' and 'passively managed' funds. An actively managed fund is one where all the investment decisions are made at the discretion of an individual investment manager, using his or her professional knowledge and experience to decide which investments to own in the fund.

A passively managed fund, in contrast, is one whose choice of holdings is determined by a pre-set formula, designed not to beat a particular market's performance but to match it. For example, a UK tracker fund would aim to replicate as closely as possible the performance of the FTSE 100 or FTSE All-Share Index.[9] These funds are run by computers according to a pre-set formula with only a tiny amount of human oversight.

Passive funds come in two main forms. The first are conventional unit trusts/OEICS which simply track a given index. Like all open-ended funds, the units are issued and redeemed by the fund provider, with orders executed on either a daily or (less commonly) a weekly basis. The second kind are known as exchange-traded funds, or ETFs for short. Unlike conventional tracker funds, these can be bought and sold just like a share in the secondary market, which makes them of interest to traders as well as long-term investors. ETFs typically offer an even wider range of choices than conventional funds, giving investors a wide variety of options for tracking individual market sectors (e.g. telecom or pharmaceutical shares as a group) as well as broader stock and bond market indices.

Having said that one of the main reasons for choosing an investment fund is that it gives you access to professional investment skills, it might seem odd that people invest in funds run by computers. Thirty years ago nobody would have thought

---

9   The FTSE 100 index tracks the performance of 100 of the largest companies on the stock market. The FTSE All-Share Index tracks more than 600 companies, including therefore many smaller companies.

that it made any sense at all. But times change and it is very much part of modern investment practice.

The awkward fact remains that there is some overwhelming evidence that most professionally managed funds don't do as well as they should. Thousands of studies have shown that if you measure how investment funds perform in aggregate, the average fund in any sector fails to do anything like as well as you might expect. By that I do not mean that the funds fail to make money – most do in the end, at least if you own them long enough. What I mean is that most funds fail to beat what experts regard as the appropriate benchmark for measuring their success or failure.

If a fund is investing in UK shares, for example, it is reasonable to suggest that over a period of a few years that fund should make more money than the UK market for shares, on average, has done. Since you can now easily buy a passively managed fund that will closely replicate the UK stock market index at relatively little cost, there is no point in paying more for an actively managed fund with the same objective if it then fails to do as well. This so-called 'benchmark' test is one that applies to all kinds of funds, whatever their investment style, and wherever they happen to choose to invest. (A North American fund should be compared to a North American benchmark, a Japanese fund to a Japanese index, and so on – that is what 'beating the market' means.)

So why do the majority of funds fail to beat their respective benchmarks? Surely any professional should be able to do better than the market average? One reason is that the costs a fund incurs when the manager actively chooses investments are much higher than if a fund is following a passive strategy. Those costs are ultimately paid for by the fund investor and reduce his or her return. So even if the manager does succeed in matching his benchmark, the costs incurred may still mean that the investor in the fund is no better off at the end of the day.

Another reason is that every fund that beats the market average has to be matched by one that does not. That is just a simple fact of life, because managing funds is what academics call a zero-sum game. Not everyone can do better than average. I comment further on this important issue in chapter 8. While passive funds certainly have their uses, I believe that the case for choosing actively managed funds still remains very strong, provided of course – and this is the important caveat – that you really understand how to pick the best ones. If you don't feel able to do that, then a passive fund is worth looking at as a sensible alternative.

Income or capital?

A second important distinction that comes out of the Investment Association classification is between funds whose primary objective is **capital appreciation** and those whose primary objective is generating **annual investment income**. Most types of fund in practice pursue a mixture of the two, and over time you will hope to get both income and capital gain from your fund. In fact, I believe that you should always think about funds in terms of what is called their total return – the combination of income and capital gain that they are likely to produce.

Nevertheless it is important to be clear what level of income any fund you are considering is likely to produce. Funds pay income to investors in the form of a dividend, typically twice a year.[10] The fund's yield is a figure that shows what percentage of the value of a fund is paid out as dividends each year. A fund that pays out £5 a year as dividends for every £100 invested in it is said to have a yield of 5%. This is important when deciding in which sector a fund should be classified. For example, the requirement for a fund to qualify for the UK Equity Income sector is that it should have a yield which is at least 10% higher than that of the stock market as a whole, as measured by the FTSE All-Share Index.

So if the stock market's aggregate dividend yield is, say, 3%, then the income fund needs to pay out at least 3.3% to qualify (110% of 3% is 3.3%). We can say that an equity income fund, therefore, is aiming to pay more in the way of income each year than the stock market as a whole pays in dividends. The flip side of this, however, is that this higher income return may come at the expense of a slower rate of capital growth.

In practice many funds allow you some choice in how you take the gains that your fund makes. They do this by offering you a choice between income and accumulation units. As their name suggests, income units pay you out any income that the investments have generated in the course of a year. Accumulation units on the other hand take the income you could have received and reinvest it in the fund itself on your behalf. That way you are effectively voting to make growing your capital, rather than generating income, your priority. You can always switch from one type to another as time goes by.

---

10   Some funds pay dividends quarterly.

Tag confusion

It is easy to be confused by the fact that funds may have more than one class of unit. This problem arises because fund companies are willing to charge lower fees to professional firms who buy large amounts of units. For some reason fund firms give different labels – usually a single capital letter – to these different kinds of unit. There is no standard method of classification, so one company will tag their retail units with, say, the letter R while others will use B. Don't ask me why! Following a change of industry rules in 2013, you also need to distinguish between 'unbundled' and 'inclusive' funds. Where you can see a choice between the two, go for the 'unbundled' one, as it will be cheaper. This kind of fund does not automatically include the payment of commissions to advisors and other intermediaries, which was standard practice before the rules were changed.

Criteria for classifying funds

Lets go back to the basic breakdown of funds by type. A quick analysis shows that two thirds of UK-registered funds on offer to investors are funds that invest predominantly in the UK equity and bond markets. That also makes it a logical place to start for any first-time investor. This is not because the UK stock market is a particularly strong reflection of what is happening in the UK economy. On the contrary, many companies listed on the UK stock market – especially the larger ones – are global businesses that only carry out a fraction of their business in the UK.

Nevertheless the UK market is a good place to start, for both equities and bonds. Among other things, UK funds are always priced in sterling, which means that you have no need to worry about movements in exchange rates when deciding where to invest. As a general rule it makes good sense, I believe, to start your investing career in your home country. Once you have started out, gained some experience and have seen how you are faring, then it could be time to start looking further afield.

My main piece of advice at this stage is simply that it is more important to pick the best funds in whichever sector you choose to look than it is to try and base your decisions on picking the best sectors first and then finding the best funds in each one. This raises the question of what makes a good and a bad fund. This is the $64,000 question. Identifying a good or a bad fund is not a simple matter. There is no single factor that makes one fund good and another bad. Rather it is a question of looking at a wide range of different criteria and forming an overall judgement as to which ones best serves your purpose and your appetite for risk.

Here are some of the factors that I think should be at the forefront of your mind when you are trying to make a judgement about funds. I return to each of these topics in more detail in the next chapter.

Performance

How much money has the fund manager made in the past? Clearly this is an important factor, but not on its own decisive, or even the most important thing to think about. There is a reason why regulators insist that every fund advertisement has to say in bold letters that **"Past performance is no guide to the future"**. It happens to be partly true. Performance is just one of several factors to take into account. You have to analyse the track record of a fund very carefully before you can assume that it will continue to do as well. Good performance in the recent past may only mean that a fund manager has been lucky. When driving, looking in the rear-view mirror is necessary, but you wouldn't want to rely solely on what you can see behind you. It is the same with investing in funds.

Risk

Some funds are riskier than others. Mainly this is because the area in which they are investing happens to be inherently riskier than those where other types of fund are investing. So, for example, funds that invest in shares are usually riskier than fixed-interest funds, and funds that invest in countries like Russia or Brazil are riskier than those which invest in the UK or United States. This tells you nothing about the skills of a fund manager. What it tends to mean is that when share prices generally are rising, a higher-risk equity fund will do better than the average, but less well than the average when the market is falling. As an investor you want to make sure that you understand and are comfortable with the risk that a fund is taking.

Investment style

Fund managers vary quite a lot in the processes they use to identify investments to include in their funds. Some are value investors, looking for shares or bonds that appear cheap against some absolute or relative metric. Others are more interested in finding shares with above-average growth potential. Some funds concentrate on larger companies, others on smaller companies. These styles will move in and out of favour, flattering the results of funds that follow the in favour styles. What you are looking to find are fund managers who can do consistently better than others *who follow the same approach*. There is not much point comparing funds with different styles.

Experience

Experience is one of the most important criteria. Investment is one of the few areas of professional life where you can clearly say that the best get better with age. The mistake that many people make is to look at how a fund is doing over too short a time period. Because markets and investment styles move in cycles that last several years, my view is that it is almost possible to judge how good an individual fund manager is until you have seen how he or she has fared over at least *two* of these cycles. In practice that means that you need to look at ten years of performance (and ideally even more).

That is what I do, taking into account the fact that the manager may have changed employers over that time. It is his or her track record that matters, not the fund when it was under somebody else's control. That is also why most of the funds that I own are run by managers who have been around quite a long time.

Fees and other charges

I have already mentioned how important the cost of your investments can be in determining the final value of your investments. Every 0.1% extra in cost you pay each year for a fund potentially reduces your annual return by the same amount – and those costs will compound remorselessly over time. All funds charge you what is called an **annual management charge** (or AMC), which is calculated as a percentage of the current value of your holding. A typical annual management charge is around 0.75%, meaning that for every £1,000 you have invested in a fund, the fund manager will deduct £7.5 a year in charges. As your fund holding grows in value, so too will the amount you pay, on a pro rata basis – so if the fund doubles in value, so will the amount you pay. In addition to the annual management charge, funds can also bill you for a number of additional costs, such as custody, although the extent to which fund companies do this varies enormously. The AMC and the additional costs together go to make up the **ongoing charges figure**, or OCF, of a fund. Some funds also charge what is called a **performance fee** – an additional amount that is only deducted if the fund beats a pre-determined performance target.

Since new rules came into force in 2013, fund companies have been free to set their charges at whatever they think the market will bear. In practice there is now a huge divergence in what funds cost. Some large players in the market, including my firm, have been able to negotiate lower fees for their clients than other investors have to pay. All this means that it is doubly important to find out what the total cost of owning a fund is likely to be before you buy it. However, it does not follow that the cheapest funds are invariably the best. In the case of passive funds, which are essentially commodities, it is broadly true, but for actively managed funds, you tend to pay for what you get – the question is whether a fund manager is really good enough to command a premium rating. I offer more thoughts on this hotly debated issue in the next chapter.

Points to remember

- There are thousands of funds from which to choose.

- The industry breaks them down into several categories.

- Passively managed funds aim to match, not beat, a relevant market index.

- Actively managed funds aim to do better than that, but most fail to do so.

- Income funds have explicit yield targets; others prioritise capital gains.

- It is best to focus on total return – income and capital gains combined.

- It is more important to look for the best funds in each sector than to pick the sectors first.

- The best fund managers tend to have been around for quite some time.

- The all-in costs of a fund are important, but not the whole story.

CHAPTER 5.

How to Pick the Best Funds

CHOOSING THE RIGHT FUND FOR YOUR PURPOSES IS probably the most difficult decision you have to make as an investor. It can turn out to be more important than your broad asset allocation, crucial though that also is. I have already touched on some of the important factors to consider in the last chapter. Here are some more detailed thoughts on the various facets of distinguishing what makes a good fund from a bad one.

When reading it, you should bear in mind my earlier observation that 90% of funds on offer are probably not worth the money you are being asked to own them – but the ones that are very good are, and they are obviously the ones that you want to have.

Funds and fund companies

I believe that many people choose their investments the wrong way round. They go for a fund company first and only then decide on which fund or funds to buy. In my experience you will do better to look for a good fund first, the one that gives you the best exposure to its chosen country, sector or theme. Which fund management company runs the fund, while not at all unimportant, should be the secondary factor. The size or reputation of the company running the fund is not as important as many investors seem to believe.

It is true that some of the larger companies offering funds have higher profiles, but that does not mean that they are necessarily superior. It may just be that they spend more money on advertising and marketing – an expense which, incidentally, is ultimately paid for by you as the fund investor. Most of the biggest fund companies offer a wide range of funds, knowing that some will do better than others, but there is no guarantee that all of them will be of the same standard, as so much depends on the skills and experience of the individual fund manager. I have already mentioned the generally disappointing performance of funds offered by the big banks. Personally I have rarely owned more than two funds from the same stable.

The good news is that there is a lot of competition within the fund management industry. This means that new names are appearing all the time. Starting a fund management company can be a very lucrative business, even if it starts small. Small 'boutique' fund management companies often start with just two or three funds, typically in niche areas. Quite often they will be started by experienced fund managers who have become frustrated working within a big company environment, where they can find themselves spending more time managing other people than doing what they do best, which is making investment decisions. By setting up on their own they become owner-managers with a significant ownership stake in their business. This not only gives them an incentive to perform, but also means they are less likely to leave or be poached by other companies, something which is a constant aggravation for both advisors and private investors alike.

Boutique firms of this kind, where managers take control of their own business, are often well worth following. While the company itself may not have a track record, the fund manager running the funds usually does. Artemis and Lindsell Train, to give just two examples, both started out with little or no money to manage, but now run many billions of pounds successfully for investors. The most prominent recent example of a fund manager setting up on his own is Neil Woodford. He left the giant Invesco Perpetual in 2014 after 25 years to start his own business, Woodford Investment Management. Sanditon and Crux are two other recent examples where experienced fund managers have left to set up on their own. There is no reason why investors should not look to have both large and small groups within a portfolio.

Remember too that in some cases the early years of a new fund, if it is run by an experienced professional, are the best time to be invested. If you wait for a three-year track record to develop at the fund manager's new home, you may miss some of the best opportunities. Why is that? Because when funds are still getting off the ground, the fund managers have more flexibility to back their highest-conviction ideas. A common problem with larger firm funds is that the fund reaches such a size that it becomes more difficult for the manager to find the opportunities he could do when the fund was much smaller.

Investment style

The investment style of a fund can have a huge bearing on the performance of your portfolio, something which is not always well-understood by many private investors (or for that matter many financial advisors). One of the most important style differences between funds is that between a 'growth' and a 'value' approach. A growth manager is primarily interested in companies with strong earnings or profits growth. This typically leads them to have a high exposure to companies which pay little by way of dividends. A value manager, on the other hand, looks at companies whose valuation appears cheap when compared with its profits, cash flow, dividends or assets. This in turn often means a predominant exposure to shares with good dividends.

Value investing has the better long-term record. The trouble is that both styles can go in and out of fashion, sometimes for years at a time. Some of the time growth beats value, and some of the time – more often, in fact – it is the other way round. Figure 5.1 shows how the two different styles have swung in and out of favour since 1990. If you buy a fund with a value approach, represented here by the high-yield index, you will do better when that style is in favour, as it has been for most of the time recently.

Although value investing produces the best long-term results, you cannot rely on it doing so every year. This kind of change in performance has little to do with the skills of the fund manager. It is purely the result of a style shift.

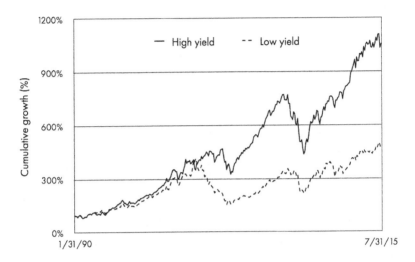

Figure 5.1. How investment styles come in and out of fashion.

It is true that some funds are blended, leaving their managers to have both styles represented in their portfolios. Their objective is then to try and vary the weight of each style, according to their reading of which style is likely to be next in favour. The difficulty is that these style shifts are notoriously difficult to time correctly. The results of getting them wrong can be painful. As a fund investor yourself, you can neutralise style effects by having both types of fund in your portfolio, but to do that requires an additional level of research. Most fund companies and platforms describe the investment approach of specific funds, while the Morningstar website classifies funds on a nine-box style matrix, designed to show the extent to which a fund veers towards large or small-cap shares and whether it is biased towards growth or value. This can be a useful starting point for further analysis.

Small caps for the longer term

The size of the companies whose shares an equity fund manager is buying needs considering because of the broad cycles that favour one or the other at any one time. At certain times so-called **blue chips**, the largest companies with household names, will perform better than small companies, and vice versa at other times. Between 1996 and 1998, for example, blue chips had a very strong run all over the world. Portfolios which were over exposed to mid-sized and smaller companies, their lesser brethren, were left lagging far behind. Then in 1999, when the valuation difference had become extreme, small companies started one of their strongest runs for years.

Since 2000, smaller companies have generally produced much stronger performance, and this has benefitted a number of specialist small-cap fund managers, such as Giles Hargreave, Harry Nimmo and Dan Nickols. Their funds have naturally attracted strong inflows on the back of their stronger performance. But that cannot continue indefinitely. Small company specialist funds, being more volatile, fell more sharply than large-cap funds during the bear market of 2007–09. And despite recovering strongly after that, since the start of 2014 smaller company funds have again mostly lagged behind.

Predicting whether large or smaller company funds will do better is difficult, so it makes sense to keep a balance between the two. Over the very long run, smaller company funds have generally outperformed larger ones, in part because they are higher-risk – when markets fall, small-cap funds fall faster and further. You might think it makes sense to have, say, 50% in larger companies and 50% in smaller company funds. However, it is worth remembering that when commentators talk about 'the market' in the UK or US, they typically mean the blue-chip indices like the Dow Jones in the United States and the FTSE 100 in the UK. If you look at the market value of the companies in those indices, they dwarf everything else.

Measured by market capitalisation, the 100 companies that make up the FTSE 100 index represent as much as 85% of the FTSE All-Share Index. The ten largest companies account for roughly 40% of the value of the index. If your portfolio only has a 50% weighting in FTSE 100 stocks, you are effectively making a big bet that smaller companies will outperform larger ones. That will work quite well a lot of the time, but in the long run you will not do as well as you expect. In practice most actively managed investment funds have a bias towards stocks outside the FTSE 100 index, so it is easy to find yourselves inadvertently making a smaller company bet without realising it. Yet again, therefore, it pays to look carefully at how and where your fund managers are investing your money.

Making sense of performance figures

This leads us on to the use of past-performance data. It is obviously right that funds should disclose as much information as possible about their past performance. For a number of years, before regulators stepped in to insist on standardised reporting of results, fund managers had much greater flexibility to present their figures in the most favourable light. Now that every company has to present its figures the same way, the risk that you will be given misleading information has reduced, although the amount of information you get may also reduce too. While that is a positive step forward, it does not mean that you are out of the woods. Interpreting past performance is a notoriously complex and difficult task.

When I talk to investors, I always stress that past performance should be only one of the tools to look at when you are considering a fund. The regulators insist that every fund has to remind investors that past performance is not a guide to future performance, and that is absolutely right. First-time investors often assume that if a fund has done well in the past, it will continue to do so. But that is clearly not the case. As we have seen, the standout feature of investment markets is that they move in cycles. Bull markets are followed by bear markets – and within each of those phases, at different times not only will smaller companies do better or worse than large ones, but some sectors will do better or worse than others and the same goes for individual companies and countries.

There are so many moving parts that determine which investments do well and which do not, in other words, that it makes interpreting fund performance highly complex. A fund that invests in smaller companies will obviously do better when smaller companies are in favour and less well when they are not. Paradoxically, the fact that it has done better than a large company fund over the past five years actually makes it less likely that it will do better in the next five years, because these style shifts tend to even out over time.

And all this is before we even consider whether the manager of a fund has added any value through his or her efforts. Suppose you are looking at two equity income funds that have exactly the same objective: does the fact that one has done better than the other over, say, the past three years tell you anything about how good the fund manager is – and just as importantly, whether or not the fund will also do better over the next three years? What if one fund has done better over one year and the other over three years? You have to dig pretty deep to come to a conclusion on which fund is worth buying.

In my experience past performance is certainly not a guarantee of future returns, but it can be a useful indicator as to when to buy or sell a fund. To take an extreme example, if the past performance figures show a fund is up by 100% in the last year, that might well be telling you to avoid buying the fund now, because in the short term what is in the fund is more than likely to be fully valued – otherwise it could not have done so well. Conversely a fund with poor performance over the previous year might just be telling you the opposite story.

In each case, you need to find out more about why performance has been good or bad. This involves asking some of these kind of questions:

- Has the fund manager made mistakes on either stock selection or asset allocation?

- Is the investment style out of sorts with the market – for example, is the fund manager a value manager when growth is taking off?

- Has a new manager been appointed with a different investment philosophy and style?

- Is the group involved in a merger? This can often mean fund managers taking their eye off the ball as they are more concerned about their own jobs.

- Has the fund become too large to be managed effectively?

Most of this information can now be found by digging around on websites, in newspapers and in the fund fact sheets you can get online through platforms. Most good websites now have charting functions that allow you to see how a fund has performed day by day, or month by month, over different periods of time. You can then compare that performance to that of other similar funds or the relevant market index. Some sites also include basic risk information, such as the volatility of returns – though not a perfect measure of risk by any means, volatility can be a useful indicator of how variable a fund's returns are likely to be.

Digging out this kind of information and processing it does take time. Putting together the whole picture is what professional analysts like myself are paid to do. At Hargreaves Lansdown we do a lot of quantitative analysis, measuring the risk and style bias of each fund in great detail. We also have the opportunity to talk to fund managers directly, which is critical – as ultimately, even when you have analysed performance figures, you are making a judgment about the ability of the individual responsible for the fund. Experience in interpreting past performance is not something that you can teach in five minutes. If you want your investments to work harder for you, it does take effort. I give some examples of the material you can find online in the appendices.

Be wary of the numbers

One of the problems every investor faces is making sure that the performance data they are seeing is actually correct. We get ours both from Funds Library, a business which collects and distributes fund reports and information, and which we own ourselves, and also from other providers. In both cases we always like to keep checking that the information is correct. That is very hard for a DIY investor to do, as they don't have easy access to, say, Lipper's professional fund research, as we do. You can, however, get pretty comprehensive fund data from the likes of FE Trustnet, the *Financial Times* and Morningstar (quite often it turns out that the information all comes from the same original source). My colleague Lee Gardhouse, who runs our multi-manager offerings, says that he quite often finds that fund companies themselves have got their performance information wrong! Given how much data there is, this may not be entirely a surprise – but it is still a fact of life that we all have to confront.

It is also very important to make sure that you are measuring performance over a long enough period to be meaningful. I have suggested that you really ought to be looking back over at least ten years of performance before you can offer a definitive judgment on how good a fund manager is. Yet finding ten-year data on a public website is very difficult. Most charting packages, for example, don't go back that far. It is equally important to track a fund manager's performance over the length of his or her career. The longer a period of outperformance, the more credible it becomes. Figure 5.2 is an example of a very long-term track record, that of Adrian Frost, the manager of the Artemis Income fund. Before Artemis launched this fund, one of my favourites, in 2002, Mr Frost had several years running a fund with the same mandate for Deutsche Bank. (This information is taken from HL's research for clients, and is not information that is visible in the fund's own literature.)

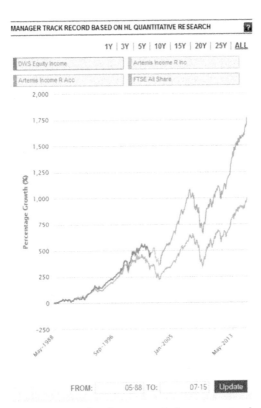

Figure 5.2: Reconstructing a fund manager's long-term track record. The example here is that of Adrian Frost, manager of the Artemis Income fund.

The 2008 financial crisis provided a classic example of how cycles can influence the typical kind of performance data that you see published. If you looked at the five-year data in 2012, the figures for most funds would still have looked terrible as the five-year period began just as we were about to go into a savage bear market. Yet by the time we reached 2014, the same funds were all showing handsome five-year performance, simply because the performance period started at the point that the market itself was recovering. The following charts give a couple of examples of this apparent dramatic turnaround in fortunes, again using Artemis Income as the example.

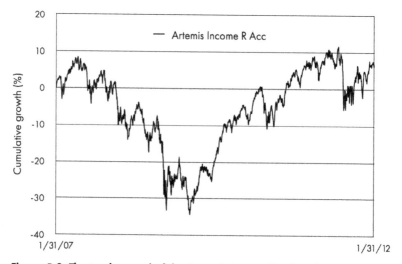

Figure 5.3: The track record of the Artemis Income fund, as it appeared in early 2012.

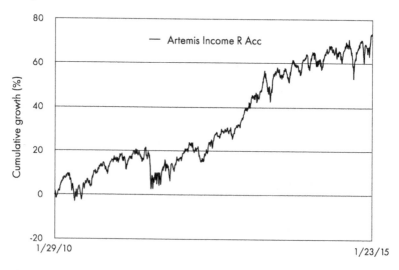

Figure 5.4: The same fund's performance record, as it appeared in January 2015.

The first chart shows the performance of the fund from January 2007 to January 2012, as it would have appeared in a five-year chart at the time. The second chart shows the performance of the fund over a different five-year period: from January 2010 to January 2015. As you can see, there is quite a difference! The second chart paints a quite different picture to the first. What it tells you is a lot more about what was happening to the stock market as a whole than it does about the fund itself. (As it happens, the fund performed better relative to the market in the first period than in the second, as you can see if you chart the whole period against the performance of the UK stock market.) So don't be taken in at first sight by how well a fund has done.

The reality is that you can prove almost anything you want if you are careful to choose the most favourable basis for your data. That is one reason why the regulators now insist that all performance data must be presented in a standardised format, although even they still say that five years is a long enough period. Newspapers are particularly prone to falling into the trap of quoting out-of-context performance numbers so as to make a good story. They are particularly fond of reporting that such and such fund manager is a new star of the industry, or alternatively has lost his touch, all based on one poor period. It even happened to Anthony Bolton, one of the most successful of all postwar UK fund managers, when he came out of retirement to run a Chinese fund in Hong Kong for his company Fidelity.

Using charts to analyse performance

Looking at performance charts, as I have suggested, can be a very helpful tool in trying to understand what funds have done and how one fund differs from another. Until quite recently customisable charts weren't readily available to the amateur investor. You could find tables of fund performance in specialist periodicals such as *Money Management*, but that was it. The internet has changed all that. These days there are scores of charting services on fund websites and all the best platforms allow you to compare funds this way. What is more, the range and quality of chart options are improving all the time.

Charts are useful because they can paint a much clearer picture of performance over time than data in a table. You can see in detail how a fund has done over a period of years – the scale of the returns, when it has outperformed and underperformed, how volatile the performance has been, and so on. It is a great way to compare funds as a good chart brings out the important differences in one simple and easy-to-grasp image. You can also compare a fund's performance against general market indices and the average performance of funds in its peer group. I have found them invaluable when answering investors who have asked why such and such a fund that appears to have done well is not on our list of recommended funds.

Once or twice the answer may be simply that we have missed a good fund, which is always possible, given how many funds there are out there. More often than not, however, I find that investors who think they have a fund which is superior to one of our own choices haven't really done sufficient homework to understand its real characteristics. Looking at charts would have made it easier for them to see the real picture. The chart below makes the point with a real-life example.

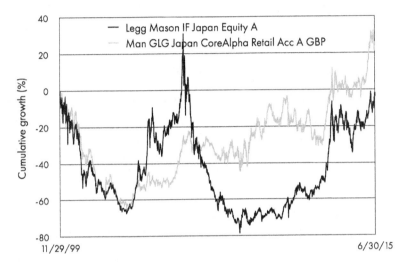

Figure 5.5: A world of difference – two Japanese funds compared.

It compares the performance of two Japanese funds, one managed by Legg Mason and the other by a company called GLG. The latter seldom appears near the top of the performance tables, while the former has been number one more than once. But which one do you as an investor really want? Clients often ask why we are not backing the Legg Mason fund. The chart gives you the answer. You can see how the Legg Mason fund made some huge gains in 2003, 2005 and 2012. If you had timed buying it at just the right moment, you would have made some spectacular gains.

But look also at how dramatically the fund fell from its peak in 2005. It was five years before it once again shot to the top of the performance table, seemingly from nowhere. The GLG fund meanwhile has been making a more prosaic journey. While it has rarely topped the short-term league tables, it has never suffered the same sharp falls either. Over the longer haul, it has been the better and more consistent performer. My conclusion is that the GLG fund is the one that I would rather own.

Note that you might never have known all this if you looked only at current performance numbers. There is a particular trap in looking at one, three and five-year cumulative performance figures. At any given point in time, such as those dates when Legg Mason Japan was shooting out the lights, all the cumulative numbers can look remarkably good. But it is important to look a bit closer. What year-by-year figures lie behind the strong cumulative performance? It may be that they reflect just one great year out of five – the most recent one. The chart will show you the real picture.

Of course, you might also draw a different conclusion from this chart. You may think that all you need to do is buy the Legg Mason fund when it is near the bottom of the performance table and sell it after it has made one of its occasional spectacular gains. Nice idea! By all means try it if you must. But don't expect me to back you to be able to do it. I wouldn't back myself to make that kind of timing call and all my experience suggests you won't be able to do so either.

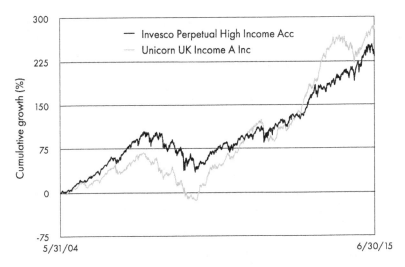

Figure 5.6: Making sense of the picture – two income funds compared.

Here is another example of the kind of insights that a chart can give you. It shows the performance of two well-known income funds, Unicorn Income and Invesco Perpetual High Income, from 2004 until the present. As it happens, both these funds have recently lost their fund managers – sadly, in the case of the Unicorn fund, as a result of the death of John McClure, and in that of the Invesco Perpetual fund, Neil Woodford's decision to leave the company to set up his own fund management business. For most of the period both funds were classified as equity income funds by the industry trade body (although for daft reasons which I won't explain here, the Invesco Perpetual fund now finds itself in the All Companies sector).

You can see that overall both funds have done very well. But note also how the journey the two funds have taken has differed. From 2004 until 2009 the Unicorn fund lagged the performance of the

Invesco Perpetual fund. Then it suddenly started to rise strongly from the bottom of the bear market in 2009. Since then it has easily performed as the better of the two funds as well as becoming one of the very top performers in the equity income sector.

How to explain that turnaround in fortune? Well, John McClure was always a good manager, well-connected and with bags of experience. What made the real difference was that after 2009 there was a huge rally in small and mid-cap stocks, one that broadly lasted until March 2014 and during which they easily outperformed large-cap stocks. It was this change in investment style which explains most of Unicorn's superior performance over this particular period. Being so much larger, the Invesco Perpetual fund inevitably had more invested in large-cap companies. There was no way that it could have matched the performance of its smaller counterpart.

Does that make it a worse fund? No. The conclusion I draw from this chart is different to the first one. While the two funds have a similar objective, the way they operate guarantees that they will fare differently in different market conditions. When small-cap stocks do particularly well, so too will the Unicorn fund. When large caps are in the ascendant, it is the Invesco Perpetual fund which is likely to outperform. None of this is difficult to grasp, but investors have to do the work to find out what is going on under the bonnet of a fund.

Charts help enormously in this respect: comparing the performance of these two funds with, say, the FTSE 100 index (as a proxy for large-cap stocks) and the FTSE All-Share or Smaller Companies indices would have quickly brought the different nature of the two funds. Unless you feel you have the skills to call the turns in investment styles, which is generally no easier than calling the tops and bottoms of bull and bear markets, it is not a bad strategy to have more than one equity income fund, each one with its own different style. I comment on this further in chapter 7.

Keeping it simple

As a performance track record can always hide things, what you want from a fund manager is a consistency of style and approach. The other day I was asked by an up-and-coming young fund manager what he should do to convince me that he had the makings of a top professional. I said, "You've got to be able to sit down and tell me what you do and what your philosophy is in no more than five minutes." It should be fairly simple. My experience over 30 years is that if the approach sounds complicated, and you have to go into a dark room and hit yourself over the head to try and understand it, then you shouldn't touch it.

In fact, if I had just one piece of advice to give anyone, it would be just that: keep it simple. What has enabled me (touch wood) to avoid most of the really bad investments I have come across over the years in financial services is recognising that complexity is normally a red flag. Investment isn't really that complicated, although a lot of professionals try to make it as complicated as possible in order to impress you with how clever they are. Neil Woodford is very good at communicating his simple philosophy and latest ideas. It is easy to understand what he is saying and he says it in about three minutes flat.

The ability to articulate what you do, simply and consistently, is what I am looking for when conducting face-to-face interviews with fund managers. I always write up my notes and do further analysis, but at heart that's what I am really after. The fund managers should be able to tell me very quickly what they do and why. Everyone can say something like, "We look to buy quality companies", and while that may sound like a great line, so what? Who is out there actually looking to buy rubbish? What we have to do is get underneath the surface and say, "What do you mean by a quality company"? The best fund managers make what they do sound like simple common sense. The ones who try to sound brilliant, usually from Oxford and Cambridge by the way, often make it more complicated for themselves!

Although it is not easy for DIY investors to get to meet the best-known fund managers in person, there are plenty of video interviews around these days so that if you start looking you can usually get to see what the person running the fund you are interested in has to say for themselves. HL carries a number of them on our website and you can also try websites like Trustnet, Morningstar and Interactive Investor. That way at least you can form a picture of what sort of person is handling your money and how well they present themselves and their story – though always remember that they will have been trained to be polished in front of a camera. (Some of them are frighteningly young, too, but most do look a bit older than the pictures in their promotional material when you meet them in person – funny that!)

All funds are required to produce regular factsheets to summarise their performance and their most important holdings. This is a useful starting point, and will include a list of the ten largest holdings and breakdown of the fund's holdings by sector. Many of the biggest firms offer visitors to their websites the facility to get email alerts about important announcements and the views of their managers. It is also possible to read the interim and annual reports of any fund. These usually have much longer pieces of commentary on a fund's objectives and performance, as well as a full list of all the holdings that a fund owns (not just the top ten). The reports produced by Artemis are among the best in this respect. Statutory reports are a very valuable information source, and one that surprisingly few investors seem to know even exist. You should definitely look for them and read them.[11]

Stick to the discipline

Once we have decided to back a manager, our primary objective afterwards is to try to make sure that they are sticking to their discipline. It is when people start to go off on a different course than the one they set out on that it starts to get dangerous. The technology boom in 1999–2000 was a classic case. For a while the craze for investing in anything vaguely tech-oriented was such that fund managers knew their careers could be lost if they failed to change course and start following the herd.

Our question to fund managers at the time was: "If you have told us at the outset that you are a disciplined value investor, only buying stocks that were cheap on valuation grounds, why are you suddenly rushing off to buy some whizzbang new company

---

11   I have included some extracts from the information that investors can dig out online about the Artemis Income fund in the appendices.

whose valuation breaks all your own rules? You wouldn't have touched it with a bargepole before." If that sort of thing happens, you know that it's all going to go wrong in the end. So anything like that is an automatic sell signal for us.

What about funds that use derivatives, which the great American investor Warren Buffett once memorably described as "financial weapons of mass destruction"? Is that a good or a bad sign? I am not necessarily against funds that use options or futures in their strategy. It all depends on how and why they use them. If the aim is simply to insure a portfolio against the risk of a severe market fall, for example, I don't mind it. Bond managers use derivatives a lot more than equity managers. Sometimes it is to get exposure to a particular type of bond or market very quickly, and that can make sense. Hedging currency exposure is also often a sensible idea.

But I don't like the call-option strategies that some of the income funds use to generate more income. That may increase the fund's income in the short run, but you never know at what cost, or whether the strategy will produce negative results in the longer term. Funds that use call options have produced a lot of income but realistically there is not much capital performance to look forward to. You have to ask if they are really suitable for the people who bought them and who may well be expecting something different.

This type of fund might be okay for people in their 70s and 80s. You could argue that at that age they are equivalent to a short-lived annuity from which you can take a thumping great income now, knowing that you won't be around to enjoy the capital after that. But would I want to do it at 55, coming up to pre-retirement planning? No, because in my view you'd be much better off with an income and growth fund at that stage.

What other professionals think

In addition to doing your own research into fund performance, there are other places where you can hope to find out more about the quality of a fund and its manager. The first and probably least useful source is to look at the ratings of funds. Fund ratings are offered by a number of specialist companies, such as Morningstar, FE Trustnet, Lipper, Square Mile and the *Financial Times*. Each one has a slightly different way of analysing a fund's performance and vary in the extent to which they apply qualitative as well as quantitative scores when assessing their rating.

In the old days funds that the ratings companies liked best were simply awarded stars, with five stars the best, rather as if they were rating a hotel or restaurant. Unfortunately at the time, before the introduction of more scientific methods, they were based largely on recent fund performance. Academic research suggests that simple star rating systems of that kind tell you little about whether a fund is worth buying now. Today, while some ratings firms still employ a star system, they tend to include a lot more data, including qualitative criteria, in their assessment. The ratings have become a lot more sophisticated. Fund rating services now look at any number of risk and return measures when calculating their risk ratings and the fund's risk-adjusted returns. The latter typically involve dividing the return a fund achieves over a certain period by the volatility (or standard deviation) of those returns so as to create a mathematical measure of risk-adjusted performance.

If you come across something called a **Sharpe ratio** or an **information ratio** in your research, they would be examples of this kind of analysis. The higher the score, the better in theory the fund. Any fund with an information or Sharpe ratio above 1.0 is said to be doing very well, while any fund whose ratio is negative is clearly doing poorly.

Why do I say that these ratings are no more than a useful starting point in determining how good a particular fund is? There are several reasons. One is simply experience. I and my research colleagues analyse a lot of the same ratios as a matter of course, but we have found that in practice they add only a little to our prior understanding of which funds are good and which ones are bad. Either they are too simple to be of any real value or too complicated to mean much beyond what you can already see for yourself in the raw performance data. However complex and sophisticated, all ratings and risk-adjusted measures also suffer from the fact that they are by definition (though to varying degrees) based on past performance data – and past performance, as we are always being reminded, is not much of a guide to future performance. Volatility of returns, although widely used as a measure of risk in financial theory, is at best a poor proxy for the real risk of a fund and at times can be positively misleading for a long-term investor. Another problem is that risk-adjusted ratios also change over time: they are not particularly stable, so a fund with a good Sharpe ratio at one point could move to a poor one a year or so later.

I suppose my conclusion to all this is: by all means have a look at ratings but never put all your faith in them. They will never be able to make up for the judgment of an experienced fund analyst.

Other useful sources

It therefore makes sense to look for guidance on which funds may be worth buying by seeking out the lists of recommended funds produced by research firms, independent financial advisors and intermediaries. The HL Wealth 150 list is an example I obviously know well, since I am responsible for producing it. The list includes our selection of the funds we like best in each of the main sectors. Other brokers also produce similar lists or reports, some of which are regularly quoted in the press. Since the Retail Distribution Review (RDR) paved the way for brokers to negotiate lower fees with fund providers, it is also worth looking around to see which advisors and intermediaries have been able to use their buying power to negotiate significant fee reductions for clients.

More often than not there can be significant overlaps between the funds that different broking and research firms recommend. This should not come as a huge surprise. Long-established fund managers with good track records, such as Neil Woodford or Nick Train, will tend to be popular with more than one research team, since most use broadly similar methods of analysis, in which past performance – whatever they may say – in practice often features prominently. In our case, we use a wide range of screening techniques to back up the information and judgments we make from our face-to-face meetings with fund managers. In particular we have developed a form of analysis that helps me to assess how much genuine stockpicking skill any individual fund manager has. That is because I believe that stockpicking skill is the key source of added value in actively managed funds.

In the bad old days before the rules changed with RDR, the situation was complicated by the fact that the choice of funds made by some brokers (not HL, I hasten to add) was heavily influenced by how much commission they stood to receive from the funds' managers. Back in the 1990s one notorious firm of 'independent' financial advisors actively invited fund management companies to bid for a place on their best buy list. Fortunately the firm was detected and subsequently forced out of business by the industry regulator, the Financial Services Authority (as it was called then).

Even if you are a DIY investor, and determined to do your own research, it is probably still worthwhile to skim through the funds that the best brokers and independent ratings companies provide. If their analysis broadly agrees with yours, that should provide you with an extra degree of comfort that the fund you have chosen has been analysed by professionals and passed at least some of their basic quality tests. By the same token if you find yourself looking at or inheriting a fund that has no rating and no professional supporters, it may be tipping you off that the fund is not really as good as it might appear. Bear in mind, though, that there may be a temptation on the part of advisors to recommend the funds where the choice is easiest to defend. (You may recall the old adage that no IT manager ever got fired for choosing IBM. I dare say something similar sometimes happens in our business.)

The third place to look for guidance on good and bad funds is in the choices made by experienced multi-managers. These are funds which only buy other funds and combine them into portfolios which they then offer to clients as one-stop solutions to the individual's fund needs. HL's range of multi-manager funds is an example and naturally draws heavily on the research work we do for the firm's Wealth 150 list. Jupiter's Merlin funds, which have been run by John Chatfeild-Roberts and his team for more than 20 years, are another well-known example.

To survive for long as a multi-manager you have to really know your stuff as your investors are paying a second layer of fees on top of the underlying fees of the funds, which can only be justified by superior long-term results. As a source of information to DIY investors, the lists of funds owned by the best multi-manager funds can, however, be invaluable. It is no surprise that almost all the funds I have in my own pension fund and ISA are those that my colleague Lee Gardhouse also has in one of his multi-manager funds.

Character and personality

In chapter 4 I make a reference to experience as a key factor in assessing fund managers. I would like to emphasise also how important character is. Fortunately no unit trust or OEIC has ever gone completely bust, or proved to be an outright fraud, but many fund managers have still done a poor job for their investors over the years.[12] They are obviously the ones you want to avoid.

---

12 The closest the industry has come to a fund default came when a notorious fund run by Morgan Grenfell proved to be investing outside its stated investment parameters. The fund's ultimate owners, Deutsche Bank, compensated the fund's investors in full.

Even good fund managers need watching: you want them to remain at all times aware that they are working for the benefit of investors, rather than just for themselves or their employers. It can happen that they simply run out of steam, or lose interest in going on with the job, although in my experience that is rare.

Business pressures may force them to become closet trackers or simply coast for a while, copying what the rest of the industry is doing, rather than thinking for themselves. Sometimes a fund management company may want or need to make sure a successful fund goes on taking in new money even though the fund has become too big and too popular for the fund manager to have any realistic hope of doing his job properly any longer. You always need to be on the alert for fund companies that are making asset gathering – raking in as many investors as possible – a priority over fund performance.

It can take time for a manager's change in attitude or motivation to become apparent. I am always on the lookout for this kind of problem when we meet fund managers, which we do on an industrial scale (300 meetings a year on average). Not every fund manager is as committed to the job as Nils Taube, who famously died at his desk well into his 70s! The great fund managers are fanatics for what they do and many also have a big financial stake in their own fund and business – always a good sign.

It is important also to remember that fund managers (at least the ones that I am looking for, managing active funds) are human beings. As such they are no different from the rest of us in having different talents, personalities and temperaments. They also differ in their personal habits, objectives and motivation. The ones I like best are those who display courage and commitment when things go wrong, as they will do from time to time. The best fund managers tend to be good under fire and never lose sight of the fact that the money they are managing ultimately belongs to you; their fund should not be solely a means to enriching themselves.

The best fund managers can earn extraordinarily large amounts of money and it is only human nature that some of them tend to ease up once they have achieved a certain level of success. As an investor you need to be alive to these risks. Having said that, most of the very good fund managers I know are a bit like kids at school. They always want to be top of the form, and this competitive urge tends to keep them going long after they can afford to quit. As professional advisors, we speak to most of the fund managers on our list on a regular basis, and keep our ears open for any hint of trouble in their personal or professional lives. That is not something that is quite as easy for ordinary investors to do, although the internet can give you some of the answers.

Costs and charges

The cost of owning a fund can have a big impact on how well it does for you. Over the last few years costs have become a greater topic within the fund industry. In simple terms it is common sense that costs must affect the final outcome of your investment, so the lower the cost the better, other things being equal. But just as you wouldn't always choose to buy the cheapest car simply because it is the cheapest, so you also need to take account of the fact that the best funds may be in a position – and justified – in charging more than those who are not so good. The critical issue is whether the result, as measured by the returns that the fund makes, more than compensates for the higher charges, taking into account also the risk profile of the fund.

Well, I hear you say, that should be relatively straightforward. But in practice it is not, because working out what the real costs of a fund are is not as easy as it sounds. One reason is that this is an area where the financial industry has hardly covered itself in glory. For many years, in the absence of a robust agreed industry disclosure standard, different companies routinely disclosed their charges in different ways, and obfuscated the figures where they could get away with it. Even now, while the industry regulator has introduced new rules on transparency and insisted on standardised reporting, there are still differences in the way that charges are set. Individual funds remain free to set their annual management fees at a level which they think the market can bear. They all charge industry professionals who can afford to buy in bulk lower fees than those you as an individual investor will be asked to pay. The amount of add-on costs that firms add to their basic management fee also varies considerably from one fund to the next.

The overall effect is that costs remain a recipe for confusion – and that is before you have to take into account some other issues that are inherent in the nature of investment, not necessarily the fault of the funds themselves. For example, if you are working out a cost figure for a particular fund, should you take the actual figure that it paid last year – or should you take the figure that is likely to incur this year? This might be quite different if the fund has grown or shrunk significantly in size over the course of a year, as can easily happen. All funds today are required to publish something known as their OCF, which stands for **ongoing charge figure**. It is the total amount that the fund spent on a range of specified costs in its last accounting period, expressed as a percentage of the size of the fund. For an actively managed fund, these will typically fall in the range of 0.5% to 2.5% per annum (though much less for a passive fund). But you should certainly not take that figure as gospel truth, for the reasons I have mentioned. For example, the additional costs (over and above the standard ones that the regulator has specified) charged by fund firms can range from nothing to as much as 0.3% in some cases.

The important point to remember here is that even small percentages can make a huge difference in cash terms. Just as positive investment returns start to grow exponentially to large amounts over the course of many years, so too will the 'cost drag' of an over-expensive fund. Over ten years, the negative impact of a 0.5% differential in fund costs can be substantial. Suppose you have two funds that both grow at the rate of 8% per annum, but one has an annual ongoing charge ratio of 1.5% and the other 1%. After ten years the difference in costs will have taken away roughly 10% of your overall gain. If you invested £10,000 in each fund at the outset, the more expensive one will have left you with £1,000 less than the other one!

So what can one sensibly say about costs? The first thing is simply to recognise that they matter, and make a point of looking at what any funds you are considering charge. Secondly, what you will find is that different types of investment fund tend to have different cost structures: in general, passive funds will (and definitely should) be the cheapest. Investment trusts and unit trusts will cost more, but their charges will be not dissimilar, although some of the older, established generalist investment trusts do tend to be cheaper than their unit trust/OEIC counterparts. Thirdly, look out for those additional costs that I have already mentioned. Fourthly, watch out also for funds and investment trusts that impose a performance fee as well as the annual management charge.

In my view, performance fees, while they may sound like a good idea, are opaque, difficult to understand and almost impossible to work out in advance, which should be enough to convince you that they are not for you. The argument you will hear for performance fees is that as they are only incurred if the fund beats a certain pre-agreed target return, they are a win-win for both investors and the fund managers. Sometimes you also hear companies say they are an added incentive for the fund managers to perform. I don't buy those arguments at all. The one thing we know about performance fees is that you pay them if the fund does well, but they don't give you your money back if the fund does poorly. In the most extreme cases, if the performance fees are uncapped, the investor can end up paying more than 4% per annum – try compounding that over ten years and then try justifying it! Performance fees, as far as I am concerned, are more about greed than anything else.[13]

---

13   I make an exception of the Woodford Patient Capital Trust, which daringly charges a performance fee but has no annual management charge at all – funny that nobody else has copied him down this path!

Where I do agree is that the real litmus test with costs is whether the fund is good enough to justify above-average management fees. I suspect that the fees on the small selection of funds which I own and recommend to clients have slightly higher-than-average annual management fees, but I certainly won't be selling them just because of that. You might think from reading the media in the last few years that the costs of funds are still very high compared to what they were years ago. The reality is that in some cases they are, but the general trend seems to be down. When I first started, most unit trusts had initial fees of 5%; for every £100 you invested, the fund took £5, partly as a set-up fee and partly to pay commission to the advisor who recommended them. Initial fees are virtually non-existent today, thank goodness. The annual fees of passive funds have also dropped a long way over the last few years. When Virgin launched one of the first All-Share tracker funds in 1996, it made much of the fact that its annual 1% management charge was cheap (which it was, but only in relative terms). Today you can buy an equivalent tracker fund for as little as 0.09% or less, so if cheap is what you want, that is the place to start.

As far as actively managed funds are concerned, they obviously charge a lot more than passive funds. The biggest change since the rules were changed in 2013 is that funds no longer automatically pay an annual commission to advisors who buy their funds for clients. Most funds used to charge investors an annual fee of 1.5%, of which half was given to the broker, advisor or intermediary who introduced the investor, and the fund management company kept the remaining 0.75%. Now funds set their own fees and investors pay whoever persuaded them to own the fund in other ways. (In industry jargon the commission payments have been 'unbundled' from the annual management charge.) The fund management companies now have to disclose their annual management fees directly, and though it is still early days since the new regime came into force I detect that the overall trend in fees seems to be gradually down.

What consumers rightly want is much greater clarity, so that they can compare the costs of funds on a like-for-like basis. The OCF has been introduced to try and help this. However, there is still a lot of argument within the industry about what should or should not be included as relevant costs. Should they, for example, include the cost of turnover within the fund (what the fund manager pays in dealing costs when buying and selling holdings)? The higher the turnover, the more it costs the fund and ultimately the consumer. It is no surprise to find that many of the very best fund managers, including many that I own, have the lowest turnover rates.

This is an evolving situation so perhaps the best thing I can say to the reader at the moment is to do further research on the subject and try and keep abreast of any potential changes. Unfortunately my experience is that many of the articles about the relative merits of passive and active investing, while they focus on costs as a key differentiator, lack balance. This is because the argument has become a quasi-religious dispute between two sets of believers who cannot accept that the other side has a point. My advice to you is to be pragmatic, seek to understand both sides of the argument and try to get the best out of both kinds of fund.

The need for patience

If there is one common mistake that I would urge investors to avoid at all costs, it is becoming too impatient with the funds they have chosen. Funds are and should be seen as medium to long-term investments; and that means giving them time to do their work. Constantly chopping and changing the funds you own because they have got off to a poor start, or are going through a bad patch, is a poor strategy. You will be much better served by taking more time with your initial selections and then sticking with them. Only if a fund consistently fails to deliver what you expect over a decent period of time should you consider switching tack.

One client recently complained to me that a nano-cap fund which has been on our list since October 2013 had done poorly. (A nano-cap fund is one which only invests in real stock market minnows, companies with a market value of less than £100 million.) I couldn't argue that the fund had done brilliantly well, as it was up only around 6%, although it had started strongly and only petered out when the small-cap rally ended in March 2014. Yet this client sold the fund solely on the basis of its short-term track record. In my view he should have been more patient, as this is the type of fund that by its nature could suddenly return 100% in a single year. The trouble is that none of us can tell you with any certainty which year that will be. With an experienced fund manager, patience usually pays off.

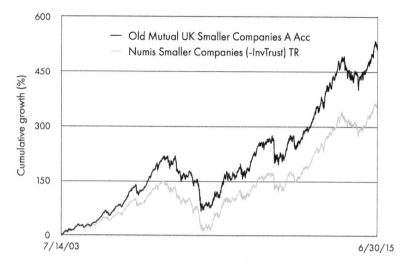

Figure 5.7: The need for patience – a smaller companies fund example.

By way of an example, take a look at these two charts, which show the performance of two actively managed funds I have followed closely for a number of years. One is the Old Mutual UK Smaller Companies fund, managed by Dan Nickols. The other is First State Asia Pacific Leaders, managed by Angus Tulloch, a long-serving member of First State's Asian equity team. Why have I picked these two funds? Because I think they illustrate very clearly how having conviction in a fund manager can pay handsome rewards for the patient investor.

Figure 5.8: The need for patience – a regional fund example.

Let's suppose you had been clever enough to see the global financial crisis coming. You could have sold these two funds in 2007 and by 2008, as the bear market intensified, you would have been feeling very smart. Both the funds lost around 50% of their value, halving your investment – no fun at all. The chances are that if you had held these funds for more than three years, you would have been nursing a loss. But when in practice would you have made a decision to buy back into those funds? Would it have been in early 2009, which (as we can see in retrospect) turned out to be the bottom of the bear market? I very much doubt it.

At the time, remember, many commentators could only see markets halving again. The media was full of talk of a double-dip recession and the risk of further bank failures. Confidence was at rock-bottom levels. Very few of our clients were buying anything.

If you had called the bottom of the market exactly at that point, you deserve your success. My point, however, is what would have happened if (as I strongly suspect) you had remained sheltering in cash. Just look at the returns that you would have missed from that low point! Remember also that if something falls by 50% in value, and you sell out, you need to make a 100% gain just to get back to where you were.

Yet both the two funds I highlight in the charts have rebounded by more than 250% from their lowest levels during the crisis. They are both comfortably well ahead of their previous 2007 highs. In other words, if you had stuck with the funds all the way through the painful crisis period, you would be now once again be sitting pretty. Those who hung on to their holdings in these two funds did not even have to make any tough decisions. The moral is clear: if you try and be too clever in timing the market, you will almost invariably lose out. Sadly I have seen it happen all too often. While holding your nerve in 2008 was not easy against a tsunami of bearish commentary, for most investors it would have been the right thing to do. All big stock market falls are followed by recovery. During the bad times, experience shows that, hard as it is, it is almost always better to hold your nerve, go fishing or whatever hobby you have that takes your mind off the worries of the world and do precisely nothing. The best funds will come back in the end.

Points to remember

- The style of a fund is a big factor behind how it performs.

- The more specialised the fund, the more volatile it will be.

- Smallcap funds are riskier, but often produce higher long-term returns.

- Aim for the best funds in each sector; don't try to pick the best sectors first.

- Always dig behind the raw performance numbers provided by your fund.

- Use charts to track the journey that a fund has made to reach its current price.

- Experience and consistency are hallmarks of the best fund managers.

- Don't be put off if fund managers leave to start their own firms; it is often a good sign.

CHAPTER 6.
Building and Managing Your Portfolio

FINDING THE BEST FUNDS AND THE BEST MANAGERS IS ONLY one aspect of your challenge as an investor. You also have to combine the funds you like into a well-balanced portfolio that fits your own goals and constraints. You want funds that dovetail well together. In this chapter I offer my thoughts on this important aspect of the fund investor's task and give examples of model portfolios that might suit a first-time fund investor. It picks up from where we left the subject of asset allocation in chapter 2.

Valuation is more important than fashion

I often hear private investors tell me that their investments have done better than professionals. I would like to think that this is true. In some cases it may be. However, those who make the claim are usually not comparing like with like. Many private investors put together portfolios that would not meet the risk constraints within which professionals are rightly required to operate, and in time this can be their undoing. They are often poorly diversified and overly-reliant on one or two individual successes that either run out of steam or can't be replicated.

This is often the case when markets start to fall, as they do periodically. The risks that people took to outperform on the way up mean that the portfolio then underperforms badly on the way down. For a while those who have struck lucky start to think that they are investment geniuses, but reality has a nasty habit of coming back to bite them. This is particularly true of investors who buy individual stocks, but applies to diversified fund investors as well. Surveys in the United States have regularly shown that private investors who buy funds rarely achieve the average fund's return (which is doubly sad as the average fund does not beat the market either). My experience in watching client behaviour at Hargreaves Lansdown over the past 15 years leads me to believe that the same pattern holds true in this country as well.

Why does this happen? The reason is that too many investors buy funds at the wrong time, usually just after those funds have experienced a period of strong performance. Investment is a cyclical business and my belief is that the way to achieve the most consistent returns is to avoid taking huge bets on which economy, sector or market is likely to perform the best in the short term. It works better to keep a foothold in all areas of the market and concentrate instead on trying to pick the best funds in each segment. There will be times when it could be right to load up on a specific style or specialist sector – but that won't be the point at which every other investor is doing the same thing. At any one time there are usually one or two sectors or markets that are being shunned by investors, typically those where the current news is bad, while others where the story and mood music is more upbeat are getting all the headlines and the positive fund flows.

With hindsight, the ones you want to buy will often be the ones that nobody else wants, not the ones that everyone else does. In practice investors tend to go for the funds that are most fashionable. Yet fashions come and go, and investors rarely spot the new trends coming and go for what is making all the waves at the moment, usually with painful consequences. During the technology boom around the turn of the century, thousands of investors made and lost fortunes by chasing over-hyped internet stocks and funds, and then failing to get out in time when the sector crashed. Dull and shunned sectors such as tobacco and pharmaceuticals meanwhile came back into favour, as did my favourite equity income funds.

Anyone who had half their money in tech funds lost out twice – first by making losses on the things they held on to for too long, and secondly by not being able to profit from the new opportunities that were going up in value while the tech sector was in meltdown. Far too few people successfully achieved the perfect outcome – riding the technology wave to its crest, selling at the top, and buying into the dip to ride the next wave, which was equity income. That is why my advice is: unless you have exceptional foresight, or are brave enough to defy consensus thinking, it is probably best not even to try and spot the next big winner.

A more prudent approach is to reduce the number of big 'bets' you make on individual sectors and markets. It is better to have a broad spread of funds across a range of different sectors in the fund universe and concentrate instead on getting extra value by choosing the best fund manager in each of the main segments. That is the approach I have followed over the years in making my own investments and also where my firm concentrates its research efforts. It may not put you at the top of the leaderboard every year – there will always be someone boasting about how well they have done in Fund X or Fund Y – but you are far more likely to come out ahead over time and avoid the below-average experience of the majority of fund investors.

Balancing risk and return in a portfolio

Clearly, when putting a portfolio together, risk should be a factor in your thinking. Risk and return usually go hand in hand – more of one, more of the other. Unfortunately risk, like beauty, is in the eye of the beholder. It is a very difficult concept to quantify. When it comes to investment, we typically mean the risk of losing your money, or some percentage of it. But does risk of loss mean that your investment is *temporarily* or *permanently* worth less than you paid for it? The former might be a price worth paying for a superior result in the longer term, while the latter would clearly not be. An alternative approach, much favoured in academic literature, equates risk with volatility, the degree to which the value of your investment varies from one period to the next.

Neither approach is wholly satisfactory, not least because understanding and tolerance for risk varies so much from one person to the next. It follows that all attempts to label investments as low, medium or higher-risk, while well-intentioned, can also be dangerously misleading. Take the example of a 'low-risk' investment, which many private investors in practice translate as meaning 'no real risk of loss'. Gilts – government bonds backed by the full force and majesty of the UK government – are often described as low-risk, but in 1994 they had their worst year for 36 years, with the price of some very long-dated gilts falling by more than 20% in just nine months. In recent years, with interest rates at their lowest level since the Bank of England was founded, and government debt at record levels, it has also been a stretch to call them safe, since anyone who buys them at current prices faces a significant risk of losing money.

In practice, risk has more than one dimension. Gilts are safe only in the sense that you are certain to get a known amount of your money back when they finally mature. But that does not mean you cannot lose money on them if you bought them at too high a price in the first place. And there is no guarantee that, when you are repaid, the value of the known amount of capital you get back will have the same purchasing power as when you began. In times of high inflation, the 'real' value of your portfolio – what you can do with the money – can be eroded very rapidly.

Another problem is that risk, as conventionally defined, is a two-way thing. It works on the upside as well as on the downside. If you are really risk-averse, it can mean that the average return you make over the years is so low that it would have been better to keep the money in the building society in the first place. One investor who wrote to me recently pointed out that his aversion to taking even the slightest risk had cost him dearly for more than 20 years. He had come to realise far too late that what he should have done, given the length of time he knew he was going to be investing, was to go for medium to high-risk investments. That way he would have stood a much better chance of producing superior returns. The general lesson is that the passage of time can turn something which looks risky in the short term into a long-term winner.

Diversification and risk

The more you dig into investment literature, the more talk you will find about the benefits of diversification, which in plain English means declining to put all your eggs in one basket. That is no more than common sense – but putting it into practice is not as easy as it once was. The key to successful diversification lies in owning a range of investments that you can reliably expect to behave in different ways to each other, so that if one is doing well or badly, another is doing the reverse. What matters, to use a statistical term much bandied about by financial advisors, is whether what you own is correlated or uncorrelated. Two funds that are positively correlated will tend to move in the same direction at the same time, while those that are negatively correlated tend to move in opposite directions.

For those who like numbers, here is table that shows you how correlated different kinds of investment assets are, based on recent experience (but be aware that these relationships can change over time). A minus sign indicates that two types of investment are negatively correlated, while a positive number suggests that they tend to move in the same direction. The closer that either number is to one (that is, +1.0 or -1.0), the greater the degree of correlation. So you can see that while the FTSE 100 index and the FTSE World Europe ex UK are highly correlated (+0.90), the same is not true of the FTSE 100 and UK gilts (-0.13). This is the argument for blending higher-risk, higher-return shares with lower-risk, normally lower-return bonds. If the stock market falls, the bonds will help to offset the impact.

10-year correlations										
	FTSE 100	S&P 500	FTSE World Europe ex UK	MSCI Emerging Markets	UK gilts	£ Investment-grade corporate bonds	€ High-yield bonds	Hedge funds	Commodity basket	UK physical property
FTSE 100	1.00	0.77	0.90	0.78	-0.11	0.47	0.74	0.72	0.46	0.25
S&P 500	0.70	1.00	0.80	0.66	0.02	0.30	0.60	0.45	0.31	0.20
FTSE World Europe ex UK	0.88	0.71	1.00	0.79	-0.02	0.42	0.82	0.65	0.38	0.12
MSCI Emerging Markets	0.66	0.68	0.68	1.00	-0.03	0.36	0.72	0.71	0.53	0.13
UK gilts	-0.16	-0.10	-0.23	-0.09	1.00	0.49	-0.05	-0.24	-0.12	-0.21
£ Investment-grade corporate bonds	0.34	0.17	0.33	0.35	0.68	1.00	0.50	0.43	0.14	0.15
€ High-yield bonds	0.74	0.55	0.86	0.69	-0.26	0.34	1.00	0.66	0.42	-0.00
Hedge funds	0.75	0.57	0.77	0.63	-0.14	0.39	0.67	1.00	0.53	0.35
Commodity basket	0.47	0.36	0.39	0.54	-0.19	0.04	0.39	0.44	1.00	0.08
UK physical property	-0.14	-0.02	-0.10	-0.05	-0.01	-0.14	-0.18	-0.00	-0.16	1.00
3-year correlations										

Table 6.1: The correlation between different types of investment.

A well-diversified portfolio will have a number of different components that tend to move in opposite directions. The table shows the correlations between various classes of investment over a recent 10-year period. A number near 1 means that two investments move in the same direction most of the time: a number near 0 implies that there is no correlation between the two, and a minus number means they move in opposite directions – making these pairs the most efficient at diversifying risk.

Source: J.P.Morgan Asset Management.

In an increasingly globalised world, however, markets and economies are much more intertwined than they were 30 years ago. It is harder, for example, to diversify geographically than it was. In the past, some countries' stock markets were not so highly correlated as they are now. A big stock market fall like the one we saw in 2008 started in the United States but spread quickly around the world. The same goes for some other types of asset: those who thought they were protected by owning corporate bonds in 2008 found that in practice there was little protection there, as they fell sharply in value too. Government bonds, cash and some types of property did provide some real defensive value during the crisis.

Fast forward and it is hard to see how, apart from very short-dated issues, government debt could do as good a job today if we were to have another big stock market setback. Cash probably remains the best general portfolio diversifier in today's markets, although interest rates are very low. It is also possible to have some diversification within each broad sector. For example, you can see from the table that UK gilts have a very low correlation with another type of fixed interest security, so-called high-yield bonds. The latter are bonds issued by companies (or countries) with relatively poor credit ratings. As such they pay a much higher rate of interest, but being much riskier than high-quality government debt behave more like equities when share prices move up and down. As a result they offer much less diversification value in a portfolio with high equity weightings, but can be a useful source of income and diversification within a bond-heavy portfolio.

Diversified and model portfolios

Everyone needs to have an element of diversification in their portfolio, to spread the risks and prepare for a range of uncertain outcomes. How you go about achieving this depends on where you are in the investment and savings spectrum. You may be just making a start on your investments and either building a portfolio gradually or looking to make a one-off initial investment which you may not be in a position to add to for a couple more years. Sometimes you may find yourself with a lump sum to invest: more common is to settle for a regular monthly or quarterly investment plan.

If you are making a one-off investment, you really want to be looking for a broad-based fund that covers all the main geographic markets. If you are starting off your investment portfolio and hope to add to it over the years, I believe that you should probably start off with a mainstream UK based fund as a core holding. You can always add a global equity fund, and the appropriate fixed-income funds for balance, at a later stage. With a more mature investment portfolio, it is easier to achieve better diversification from the beginning, even if it means reorganising what you already have. It makes sense as time goes by to look to blend one or more funds within each broad asset class that have complementary rather than identical strategies.

It is no coincidence, incidentally, that very few asset management companies have been able to add value consistently for their clients by making frequent asset-allocation decisions from one period to the next – in other words, changing the mix between shares, bonds, property and so forth on a regular basis. I see little evidence that most investment groups add value this way, and I certainly would not encourage you to do so. There are always some exceptions to this rule, but in my experience not many. For example, most professional investors were selling their bonds in 2010/11, yet bonds continued to be a great place to be right up to 2015.

As a general rule I believe that your bias should be towards making as few big calls as possible. Most big asset-allocation moves by investors tend to be knee-jerk emotive reactions to headline-grabbing events that are either happening elsewhere in the world, such as Greece or China, or are political rather than financial in nature, such as general elections. Most of the time these 'critical' events turn out to be more benign than they seem at the time. If anything, widespread fear of this kind of event can provide good entry points for topping up your holdings. They reflect emotions, not fundamentals. Sharp stock market falls are normally best seen as opportunities to buy, not to sell.

It is true that from time to time asset classes do become very expensive or very cheap when measured against their long-term history. It is here that knowing and understanding a bit of its history can help in terms of the valuation of a major asset class. But this only happens once or twice in a decade. The majority of the time asset classes are in no man's land. This means they can move either up or down by 20%, but nobody really knows which way and trying to guess is more akin to gambling. It is better to sit still instead. Go and play a round of golf, go fishing, sailing or whatever your pastime is!

Without knowing each individual reader's personal circumstances, it is impossible for me to give specific advice about which individual funds are right for you. However, it may be worth taking a look at some of the starting model portfolios which I have designed for clients of HL. There are five main types in all.[14] The key determinants are how much an investor has to invest, whether they are investing a lump sum or on a regular basis (so much a month, quarter or year) and crucially their time horizon and tolerance for risk. While each individual case is different, these are designed to be benchmarks against which you can usefully measure your own situation. The minimum requirements are either a lump sum of £100 or a regular monthly investment of £25. To keep things consistent, in the examples I have gone for similar investment assumptions in each case – a lump sum of £10,000 a year, or £500 a month.

Figure 6.1: Conservative portfolio

---

14   Conservative, medium risk, adventurous, investing for children, and regular income.

This is the portfolio I might suggest for someone who is not able or willing to take on much investment risk – perhaps because they have little money to spare, or because they feel they will need the money they have invested in a relatively short period of time. The portfolio consists of four very conservatively managed funds which will never make huge positive returns, but are likely to suffer much less if and when the stock market turns down. The money is split equally between the four funds. (Note how the class of units mentioned here all have different letters, even though they are all directed at ordinary private investors – an example of how the industry continues to confuse people needlessly!) If you drilled down into what these four funds own, you would find a high percentage in bonds and fixed-interest securities.

Figure 6.2: Medium-risk portfolio

Here is an example of a medium-risk portfolio for an investor looking to invest a lump sum of £10,000. This one has five funds in it. Two of those five, Newton Real Return and Artemis Strategic Assets, are also found in the conservative portfolio. The other three funds inject more equity exposure into the portfolio. Woodford Equity Income, Old Mutual UK Alpha and Lindsell

Train Global Equity all invest in shares of companies, though mostly in the largest companies in either the UK or global markets. The other two funds invest in a mixture of shares and bonds, with the primary aim not of maximising returns but seeking to perform steadily through all kinds of market conditions. Because of the large number of holdings which each of the five funds has, the portfolio is very well-diversified, both geographically and by type of asset, even though there are only five names in it.

Figure 6.3: Adventurous portfolio

For someone with a greater appetite for risk, a more appropriate starting point might be the adventurous starter model portfolio, which looks like this (as of May 2015). Again, two of the funds are the same as those in the medium-risk portfolio, but now there is a much greater exposure to emerging markets and smaller companies, which tend to perform better over longer periods of time, despite their higher risk. The Marlborough Micro-cap fund, which invests in quoted companies drawn from the smallest segment of the market by value, has only a 10% weighting for that reason. As the markets ebb and flow, you would expect this fund to move higher and fall further than the other two portfolios.

Figure 6.4: A portfolio for children

This portfolio is one designed specifically for children whose parents have decided to put aside money on their behalf. The logic here is that children have a long investment life ahead of them, so it is appropriate to take a maximum amount of equity risk, as we have seen how the passage of time increases the likelihood that equities will deliver strong positive returns. Children probably won't have access to these investments until they are 18 or 21, and potentially their investment horizon could be even longer. They have plenty of time to let their investments mature. As a result the portfolio includes a much higher weighting in emerging markets (40% in the Newton and First State funds) and also 20% in one of my favourite small-cap investment funds.

Figure 6.5: A portfolio for regular income

The final portfolio is designed for those who specifically want an income from their investment portfolio, with capital growth as a secondary objective. The bulk of the portfolio is made up of the HL multi-manager income and growth trust, which invests in 11 of the equity income funds that the firm rates most highly. (This is a fund that I also own in my personal portfolio.) The other two funds invest exclusively in fixed-interest securities, though their investment approaches are different. The Royal London fund pays out more in income, and is consequently higher risk, than the Artemis Strategic Bond fund, which has more flexibility to protect its capital if the bond markets turn down – provided the manager makes the right decisions of course. This is a good example of how it is possible to achieve diversification within particular asset classes, and not just between them. Together they provide a more rounded exposure to the fixed-interest market.

Going back to the medium-risk portfolio, it is worth pointing out that while it has no bond funds as such, that does not mean that there is no diversification protection built into it. You always have to look deeper into what a fund owns to discover its real nature. The Newton Real Return fund, for example, has 37% in bonds and 7% in cash, while Artemis Strategic Assets has about 25% in cash and equivalents. In reality the Artemis fund is heavily shorting government bonds across the developed bond markets like the US, UK and Japan, which means it will do well if those bonds start to fall in value.

You will notice that I have mostly used the same funds as building blocks for all these portfolios. They happen to be the ones that I have researched very thoroughly and know very well. My analysis also suggests that they will blend well together, which is another crucial factor. Other professional investors and advisors might well recommend different funds as building blocks. There is nothing to say that only these specific funds will do the job required of them. I could suggest one or two credible alternatives for most of the portfolios. However, the important point is that the great majority of actively managed funds will not beat the market averages: and unless they do, you might as well as use a series of cheaper index funds instead. The challenge – and the rewards – come from finding the small number of exceptional fund managers in each of the main sectors.

Weightings and fund numbers

It is important to emphasise that you do not have to be bound by the precise weightings I suggest for each portfolio. You can choose to keep some money back as cash, or change the weighting given to each fund in your portfolio – which you might want to do in order to change the overall risk of the portfolio. The same is true of the number of funds you invest in. For portfolios of £10,000 you won't benefit from having more than three or four funds in your portfolio. With larger sums you can afford to spread the money across more funds, which has the effect of reducing your specific fund manager risk. So for example, for a medium-risk portfolio of £200,000 I suggest increasing the number of funds from five to seven, as shown in figure 6.6. With larger sums you might want to up the number to the 15–20 range, but you will rarely need more than that number, even if you have millions to invest.

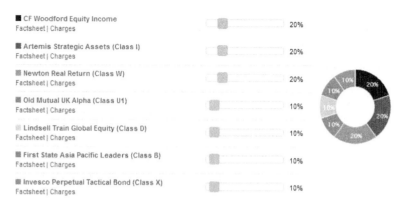

■ CF Woodford Equity Income
Factsheet | Charges   20%

■ Artemis Strategic Assets (Class I)
Factsheet | Charges   20%

■ Newton Real Return (Class W)
Factsheet | Charges   20%

■ Old Mutual UK Alpha (Class U1)
Factsheet | Charges   10%

■ Lindsell Train Global Equity (Class D)
Factsheet | Charges   10%

■ First State Asia Pacific Leaders (Class B)
Factsheet | Charges   10%

■ Invesco Perpetual Tactical Bond (Class X)
Factsheet | Charges   10%

Figure 6.6: A medium portfolio for investors with larger sums to invest.

There is nothing to stop you adding more risk by adding new funds later on. For example, if you wish to make the medium-risk portfolio more aggressive, you could increase exposure to the Far East and emerging markets yourself. Alternatively you could switch the UK allocation towards smaller companies or specialised funds that focus on particular sectors, such as financials, technology and healthcare. For those seeking a more cautious approach, you could increase the amount dedicated to fixed interest. An allocation of 15–20% to bonds will tend to reduce the volatility of the portfolio.

However, you will also need to look at what level of income you are getting. If yields on corporate bonds are down to low levels historically, you may do better to retain a higher cash position, switching a bigger chunk of your money into your bank or building society account instead. I should stress again that these model portfolios are suggestions to help investors to get started. You will see similar models on other websites and platforms. They are best used as a baseline. Add or subtract other funds according to your personal tolerance for risk.

Rebalancing

An important issue that you need to think about is whether or not to rebalance your portfolio at regular intervals. Rebalancing is a term that means taking steps to ensure that your asset allocation – how your portfolio is made up as between different asset classes or types of fund – remains the same over time. For example, suppose that you set out with the aim of creating a portfolio that is 60% invested in equities and 40% in bonds. A year later, equities have gone up by 20% while your bond funds have produced a 5% return. The relative weights of the two types of investment in your portfolio have therefore changed too.

The following table shows how the figures would now look. As you can see, even without you doing anything, the equity portion of your portfolio has risen from 60% to 64.3%, purely as the result of the difference in performance between the two categories. The greater the number of years that you leave your portfolio to take its own path without rebalancing, the further away from your original target it is likely to take you (although some years the process will even out if the performance gap between equities and bonds reverses).

Start of year				End of year	
Holding	Invested	Weighting	Return	New total	Weighting
Equity funds	£6,000	60.0%	20%	£7,200	63.2%
Bond funds	£4,000	40.0%	5%	£4,200	36.8%
Total	£10,000	100.0%		£11,400	100.0%

Table 6.2: How your asset allocation can change as time goes by.

The question is whether it makes sense to return your portfolio to its original target weights, or whether you simply let things take their natural course. If you decide to rebalance, you would look to take something from the equity side of your holdings and increase the bond allocation with the proceeds. You would sell enough units in the equity holding to reduce them to an amount equivalent to 60% of the new overall total of £11,400. This would leave you with £6,840 in equities and £4,560 in bonds, as per the table below. The following year you would repeat the exercise.

End of year							
Holding	Units	Value	Per unit	Required	Action	Holding	Weight
Equity funds	6,000	£7,200	£1.20	£6,840	Sell 300	5,700	60%
Bond funds	4,000	£4,200	£1.05	£4,560	Buy 342	4,342	40%
Total	10,000	£11,400		£11,400		10,042	100%

Table 6.3: An action plan for rebalancing your portfolio.

Rebalancing can be done at any time, but many investors who follow this course typically do it once a year. The first advantage of rebalancing is that you know that your risk profile will stay broadly the same from one year to another, something that becomes more important as time goes by. At the same time, you are selling the funds or asset class which have done best and buying the ones which have not done so well. Surprising as it may sound, this is a second reason why rebalancing might be a good idea. Selling outperformers and buying underperformers is not at all a bad investment strategy, although my experience is that investors often do the opposite. I remember one portfolio review meeting with a client. Having congratulated myself on how well his portfolio had done beforehand, I imagined that our meeting would be quite congenial. Far from it. He berated me for the funds in the portfolio which had done poorly and wanted me to sell these and buy the ones that had done well.

As I tried to explain to him, doing what he was suggesting is almost always a mistake, because loading up on past winners destroys the diversification value that comes from owning a balanced portfolio when things go ugly. Many people found out the dangers at the height of the internet boom in February 2000. I remember one client who rang our office and insisted on selling all his equity income funds in order to switch into the TMT (technology, media and telecom) funds that were all the rage at the time. We said: "Are you sure?" His reply was, "I have a strict discipline of selling my losers and buying the winners". Of course, it all then went horribly wrong and he lost a packet when just a few months later TMT funds dropped like a stone and equity income funds soared.

By upping his holdings in funds that were already showing such exceptional gains, he was ensuring that his portfolio was becoming even more skewed in just one direction. It was no longer even remotely balanced. Rebalancing at the start of 2000 would have saved him a fortune. The point is that following a mechanical rebalancing discipline at regular intervals can stop you falling prey to your emotions. Investors always find it hard to sell things that have gone up a lot. They are terrified of leaving money lying on the table by selling too soon. But it is often the right thing to do. Rebalancing in that sense is a means to saving you from yourself.

There is a downside, of course. Every time you sell some funds to buy others, you incur dealing charges, and the more often you do it, the greater the cost becomes. That was a bigger problem a few years ago, when many funds still charged you 5% upfront as a buying fee. My view is that it can be sensible to do some rebalancing of either assets or funds themselves, but I don't think it is essential when you have more experience. Whether it should be done on a particular anniversary every year, such as January the 1st, I rather doubt. I like to look at the wider picture of what is going on in the markets and economies before binding myself to a particular date in the calendar and I suspect that once a year may actually be too frequent an interval.

Keeping an eye on the shape of your portfolio over time is, however, obviously common sense. It is important to beware of double counting. Fifteen years ago many investors bought specialist technology funds without realising that the other funds they owned were already investing heavily in the same space. Some European equity funds, for example, had more than 50% in the tech sector. When the technology craze passed, those investors suffered a double whammy of losses.

What this underlines is that while adding more funds to your portfolio helps to protect you, having say five funds which are all doing the same thing is a waste of time. If you own equity income funds, it makes sense to have both Artemis Income and the Marlborough Multi Cap Income, for example, as they invest in different sectors of the equity market. But it makes little sense to pair two equity income funds that are doing more or less the same thing. The same goes for bond funds. It is sensible to pair a high-yield fund alongside an investment-grade fund, but not to have two that are cut from the same cloth. Once again you have to look under the bonnet to find out what you have. A number of platforms offer so-called x-ray tools that help you to find this information out.

Themes and sectors

The onset of globalisation in recent years means that ensuring you have a finger in all the main types of fund is more difficult. For example, a company like Glaxo is listed in the UK, but the vast majority of its profits come from America, so which country is more important to its results? Shell, the doyen of the oil sector, operates right around the world and reports its dividends in dollars, not pounds. If you are seeking to analyse your geographical diversification, which stocks should you include where? The past few years have seen a large number of new sector and theme funds being launched. There is nothing intrinsically wrong with this, but it can easily cause you to over-concentrate your portfolio in one area of the market.

For example, buying a fund that only invests in financial stocks may not be necessary if you already have other unit trusts with a significant weighting in financial stocks. You should weigh up carefully the make-up of your existing portfolio holdings before stuffing it with additional sector/theme funds. My experience has been that if you do buy a specialist fund and it does well over say a two to three year period, then you should consider selling it, as individual themes and sectors rarely continue to outperform indefinitely. This is the opposite of what I suggest you do with your core diversified holdings, where it is worth holding on and backing a good fund manager through occasional poor periods.

The more specific the investment objective of a fund, and the riskier the underlying holdings, the more dramatic the movements in its price are likely to be. Two exceptional examples in recent years would be gold and Russian country funds. Take a look at this chart of the Blackrock Gold & General Fund, probably the most popular of all the specialist funds investing in gold and mining shares. For ten years after the turn of the century, the fund produced some stellar returns, albeit interrupted by a dramatic collapse during the financial crisis of 2008. By Q1 2011 investors who had bought the fund six years earlier were sitting on gains of more than 300%.

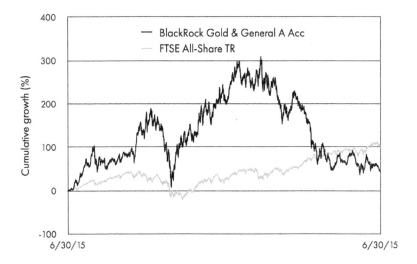

Figure 6.7: A roller-coaster ride – the Blackrock Gold & General Fund.

The manager is a talented individual, but even he was unable to keep performance going when the resources boom that had driven mining stocks sharply up in value for several years started to reverse. Loyal investors were caught on the hop as the fund fell in value by more than 60% in little over two years. Many lost all the gains that they had accumulated in the earlier period. (I know, as I was one of them, breaking one of my golden rules of investment: never fail to take at least some profits from your specialist funds as they go up.) Those who still hold the fund in their portfolios are now almost back to where they started, with little even in the way of dividends to show for their patience. Like the Duke of York, they have marched their money all the way up, and now they have marched it down again. Investors in Russian funds have enjoyed an almost identical ride – rapid gains leading up to a peak and then a relentless decline, as the next chart illustrates. It shows the performance of the Neptune

Russia fund over the past ten years, one of the few specialist funds that invests solely in Russian companies. It clearly follows the same pattern as the mining fund, with periods of outrageously good and outrageously poor performance. The reasons are not that hard to find. The Russian stock market is relatively small for such a vast country and is completely dominated, like the Russian economy itself, by oil, gas and resources companies. You would not call Gazprom, the largest company of all on the Russian stock exchange, a model of good corporate governance, since it is scarcely credible that it would ever put the interests of shareholders ahead of those of the Kremlin.

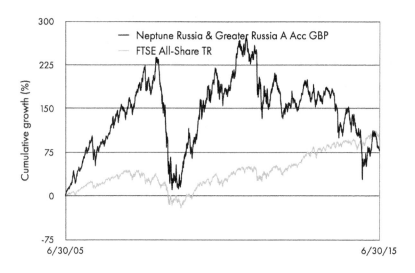

Figure 6.8: Another up and down experience – the Neptune Russia Fund.

Yet as long as commodities were still every investor's favourite investment sector, if you could stomach the various risks, you would at least have remained comfortably ahead. Since 2011, however, the trend has gone into sharp reverse. Even though the oil price remained above $100 a barrel until the middle of 2014, the Russian stock market started falling well before then – a good example of how stock markets are often forward indicators of trouble ahead. In 2014 the seizure of Crimea led to heightened fears about political stability, while the sanctions that followed naturally depressed the value of any company based in the country.

The lesson that I take from all this is not that specialist funds should be avoided completely. If you can spot a developing trend in a specialist area, there is nothing wrong in joining the bandwagon – so long as you keep a sense of reality. Funds that shoot up very fast – much faster than the market as a whole – invariably tend to give most of the gains back on the other side. What is more, the nearer they are to their peak, the more attention they will be getting from the media and advisor community, assuring you that they are the best thing since sliced bread – a good signal that you need to start being more cautious.

If you reach a point where a fund is up by 100% in one year, or by 200% or more over three to five years, my advice is that you should already be thinking about reducing your exposure. Don't worry about leaving money on the table. Bank the gain and move on to something else. As Warren Buffett likes to say, "Be fearful when others are greedy. Be greedy when others are fearful". DIY investors often seem to think that if something like gold or Russia becomes wildly expensive, the manager of a specialist fund in those areas will start to sell his holdings in favour of cash in order to wait for better opportunities ahead. But that is unfortunately not how the business works. What the managers of the funds will say is that they are being paid to own stocks in their specialist area and they are not mandated to do anything else. (The cynics among you might say that they have no financial incentive to do anything else – I couldn't possibly comment.) It is always down to you to yank your money out when the going gets too good to be true. In the industry we call this kind of fund 'sex and violence funds': the problem is you tend to get the violence, but not the sex!

Points to remember

- Portfolios are made up of a number of different funds.

- Funds that are currently fashionable are often the most dangerous.

- The objective is to match your risk profile. You can vary the risk in any portfolio by adding bonds or cash.

- Rebalancing can be a useful way to keep your risk at the right level.

- Adding more than one fund in each sector can reduce your risk – but not if the funds are doing exactly the same thing.

- Think about selling specialist funds that have shot up a long way very quickly.

CHAPTER 7.

How I Invest My Own Money

G IVEN THAT IT IS MY JOB TO HELP OTHER PEOPLE DECIDE what to do with their money, it is only fair to share with you what I do with my own money. I am lucky enough to be well-paid for what I do and have access to the work of a highly-skilled research team. But if you look closely at what I do with my own finances, there is very little in principle that you could not do yourself. If there are echoes of some of the things I have said in earlier chapters, that is because I always try to do myself what I recommend to others.

So, for example, I have for many years made full use of both the annual ISA allowance and the tax relief available on contributions into my SIPP (personal pension). The most significant investments I have outside these two tax-efficient pots of money are some holdings in venture capital trusts, which I describe in the next chapter. (They are attractive primarily because they too have tax advantages. They pay tax-free dividends, something I am looking forward to receiving when I retire.) The messages I give to others – keep it simple, stick to your principles, learn from your experiences and you won't go far wrong – are those I try to follow myself. Don't be afraid to ask other experienced investors or trusted colleagues for advice; they can be very helpful. I regularly ask my colleague Lee Gardhouse, for example, for his thoughts on funds I am thinking of buying or selling.

One important disclaimer

It is worth saying up front that one of the things that is irritating about most financial advice, whether from the industry, media or regulators, is the cosy assumption that everyone's life proceeds in a single straightforward line, untroubled by chance, unexpected events and family or career interruptions and shocks. We all know that in reality life is never really like that. While it may have been much simpler in the days when jobs were for life, and job mobility much lower, most people's careers and financial circumstances these days inevitably advance in stops and starts.

I am in my late 50s and lucky to be comfortably off. There will come a time before long when I will want to start slowing down, though whether I actually retire altogether I am not sure. Like most people who work in the investment business, I am having too much fun to be sure how I would keep myself amused without the stimulus of keeping a close eye on what is going on in the markets.

But I have not been comfortable forever – far from it. I have already described how the stock market crash in 1987 was a very tough time for me and my family financially. I was still in my early 30s and my income suffered a sharp fall when I could least afford it. Because I worked in the business, I had been smart enough to start making payments into a private pension plan, on top of the mortgage and ordinary outgoings that my wife and I had at the time. It did not take me long, however, to realise what rotten value the private pensions of those days were. They were called Section 226 schemes – and with a stupid name like that it was perhaps not a surprise that so few people were rushing to take one out.

The charges on these schemes were astronomically high. For that reason they were very popular with life industry salesmen, who could earn a huge chunk of savers' money as upfront commissions. In some cases they were taking as much as four years' worth of your regular savings as a reward! If you invested a lump sum of £25,000 in a private pension, after the sales guys had taken their cut, you were several thousands of pounds down before you even started investing. Over, say, 25 years the money they took upfront could have become a whole lot more. (To give one example, £5,000 invested in the stock market in 1990 would be worth more than seven times as much today.)

The opportunity cost, in other words, was huge. When the regulators finally forced the life companies to come clean about their charges, there was a lot of pushback from consumer groups and parliament and eventually door-to-door insurance salesmen found that their days were numbered. Don't get me wrong. Salesmen weren't all bad, in that they did at least get some people saving – but that saving could have produced so much bigger returns if the charges had been more reasonable. (Nor should you worry too much about the salesmen: many of them simply hung up their raincoats and set up shop as so-called independent financial advisors, where until the rules changed recently they continued to take thousands of pounds in sales commission under the guise of giving advice on products they were effectively being paid to promote. Not all financial advisors are poor and sales-driven only, but the question has always been integrity.)

The early 1990s, when interest rates shot up, was a tough period for everyone and it was only a few years after I joined Hargreaves Lansdown that I finally became well-paid enough to start saving regularly at the rate required to build up my income requirements for later in life. Some years I was able to put quite a big chunk of what I earned as a pension contribution into my SIPP. Unfortunately, over the last few years, the limits on how much you can contribute in any given year have been sharply reduced, in part because of the government's fears that people taking advantage of the tax breaks on pension contributions were costing them too much in lost tax revenue. For those who qualify, however, they remain a valuable incentive, as they have been for me.

A balance of ISAs, SIPPs and others

Having been able to make full use of both my ISA and pension allowances, I think of my portfolio as a single investment pot. The funds that I buy for each one are to a large extent the same. I have always taken the view that a good fund will do the same job wherever it is held. One difference is that I own a number of shares in my company, Hargreaves Lansdown, and as a result shares make up a bigger proportion of my ISA than my SIPP. But, as funds are my area of specialism, I don't as a rule own a lot of individual shares.

You can see a list of the largest investments in my SIPP on page 146. My biggest ISA holdings are shown on page 160. The similarity between my ISA and SIPP portfolios may become less marked in years to come as I gradually start to look forward to the time when I draw more from my pension fund as income, rather than continuing to try and accumulate as much capital as possible. That point will come if and when I start winding down from my job.

That may not ultimately be my decision to make – like anyone else, the company could decide I am starting to lose my marbles and ease me out – so it is obviously prudent to slowly alter the mix of funds I own in the two different pots towards a greater reliance on income-generation. This is a natural progression for anyone who is approaching retirement age. The younger you are, the more relaxed you can afford to be about the balance between income and capital appreciation (but bear in mind that funds which pay regular and rising dividends tend also to produce higher total returns over a period of years, so they can be worth opting for even if you don't take them as they are paid).

Flexibility is crucial

It is worth remembering how flexible funds can be in planning ahead in this way. I have already described the advantages I see in owning equity income funds, not just for their generally superior returns, but also because you don't need to overhaul your portfolio so radically as and when your income needs change. All you have to do at that point is switch from reinvesting the regular distributions to taking them as income.

When it comes to buying accumulation or income units, I generally prefer to opt for the income units. The main reason is that it means that I always have some new money coming in which I can invest where I currently see the best value. Sometimes a new fund launch will catch my eye. Or I may decide that there is a particular market or sector that looks particularly attractive at the time. Or I may simply want to tweak the mix of the portfolio a little bit.

In practice my experience is that the best opportunities for new investments often come when there is a sudden or unexpected market sell-off. If the equity markets fall by 10%–15%, it is usually because there is a fair amount of bad news around. That gives you a chance to pick up some more of your favourite funds at an attractive price. Good recent examples would be the succession of market scares we have had over the future of the eurozone. By my reckoning there have been at least four euro panics in the last few years that have sent investors running for cover. In each case I have used the sell-offs to put some more money to work.

Another good recent example came in September/October 2014 when the markets sold off quite sharply and I was able to add to two of my favourite holdings – both of them, for the reasons I have given, income funds. One was my old favourite, Neil Woodford's Equity Income fund, and the second our own HL Income and Growth Fund (which invests in many of our research team's favourite funds). A few years ago, in the same circumstances, I might not have put so much into income funds, and split the money somewhat differently. Another fund I bought, one which invests in more volatile emerging markets, was experiencing a particularly bad run at the time, but the manager was doing nothing different – it was just market sentiment at work, so I was happy to buy some more.[15]

The point is that as a long-term investor, confident about which funds I want to own, I can afford to take a more relaxed attitude to short-term market moves, knowing that the ups and downs of sentiment-driven market cycles will even out over time. Many first-time investors find it difficult to sit through market squalls. If everyone else seems to be selling, you have to be quite determined to want to do the opposite. Yet that is what you have to steel yourself to do. At the end of the day, investments are like everything else. The cheaper they are, the more value you will get from them. Yet bizarrely investors often seem to think that only the expensive stuff is worth buying! To remind myself of the need to stay calm during market declines, I have a sign on my desk at work which reads: *"Don't just do something, sit there!"*

With specialist funds, my thinking has changed somewhat over the years. I was one of those who enjoyed the gains from the BlackRock Gold & General fund as its value went shooting up during the commodity boom in the first decade of this century. But I have to admit that I also then hung on for far too long after the price started to decline. What I think now is that if you can spot a developing trend in a specialist area, there is nothing

---

15   Jason Pidcock, the manager of this fund, later left to join another fund management firm, prompting me to put this fund holding under review.

wrong in joining the bandwagon – just so long as you keep a sense of reality and perspective about you. If you reach a point where a fund is up by 100% in one year, or by 200% or more over three to five years, my advice is that you should already be thinking about reducing your exposure or selling out completely.

Unlike mainstream or broad market funds, where it is sensible advice to stick with your winners, you can have too much of a good thing with specialist funds. Don't worry about leaving money on the table. Bank the gain and move on to something else. I would certainly say that failing to sell specialist funds when I have already made a lot of money from them is at the top of the list of my worst mistakes as an investor. Unless you are confident you have the self-discipline to sell somewhere near the peak, you might do better to avoid the specialist sectors altogether.

The funds I own

In order, the top holdings in my SIPP and ISA (at 30 June 2015) were as follows:[16]

Main SIPP holdings

- HL Growth and Income

- Darwin Leisure

- Woodford Equity Income

---

16   Please note that I describe my thoughts on venture capital trusts and individual shares in more detail in chapter 8. They are not covered in this section, although they make up a good chunk of my overall investment portfolio.

- Marlborough Micro-Cap and Nano-Cap

- Royal London Sterling Extra Yield

- Artemis Strategic Assets

- RIT Capital Partners

- Lindsell Train Global Equity

My aim is never to have more than 10% in any one fund. A few years ago my SIPP was 100% invested, but more recently I have been gradually increasing the holdings of cash. This is partly the result of reviewing my pension plans in the light of recent legislative changes, which have changed the rules of the game for someone in my position.

These funds together make up somewhat over half of the overall value of my SIPP, with cash or equivalents around 30%. The two Marlborough funds are both managed by Giles Hargreave and his team at Hargreave Hale. While they have different objectives, I mentally count them together as my largest exposure to the smaller company universe. As I have said, the cash holding, at 30%, is very high by my historical standards.

Here are my brief thoughts on each of the funds. It is important to say that while I rarely make big changes in my personal portfolio, there is no guarantee that I will still own these funds by the time you read this book. These funds suit me, but I am not recommending that they will necessarily be the best ones for you. What I am trying to do is explain the thinking behind my owning what I do.

HL Multi-Manager Growth and Income

As my working days revolve around analysing funds, you may be wondering why there aren't more of the funds we recommend to clients in my portfolio. Well, actually, there are. The multi-manager team, led by my colleague Lee Gardhouse, is responsible for bundling the best of the funds we like into well-diversified multi-manager funds. They are aimed at clients who for whatever reason decide that they don't want the hassle of doing all the necessary fund research themselves. We now have seven different multi-manager funds, having added UK growth, European, Asia and emerging markets offerings to the range in the last year.

The Growth and Income fund, now the largest holding in my SIPP, was one of the first multi-manager funds we launched back in 2002 and it remains the largest and most popular today. I have been a regular investor since the start. What does it do? Well, by now, given my longstanding bias towards equity income funds, you won't be surprised to hear that it invests in the best equity income funds we can find. One or two of the funds in the portfolio, like the Woodford Equity income fund, are ones I also own directly. But many of the others I do not. The fund has 11 holdings in all and includes equity income offerings from Artemis, Threadneedle, Jupiter, Liontrust and First State. The historic yield is about 3.75%, while the capital value of the accumulation units has risen by around 80% over five years.

Darwin Leisure

People are always surprised to find this virtually unknown fund near the top of my list of holdings. They are even more surprised when they find out what it does, which is invest in a portfolio of caravan parks. What could be less glamorous or mainstream than that? To be honest, even I never expected this fund to do so well when I first bought it over a decade ago. But it has done me proud ever since then.

The fund is effectively a kind of family unit trust. What the fund does – and what makes them different – is buy, manage and then improve their caravan parks. Most caravan parks don't do improvements. The owners take the income but rarely invest in making them more attractive places to stay. I have one down the road from me and I have seen the difference that their investment makes. Their sites are closer to chalets than what most of us remember caravan parks being like. That in turn attracts a more upmarket kind of visitor – more Center Parcs than *Carry On Camping*, if you like.

It has become a fantastic business, which is what this fund really is. The fund yields about 6.5% and now they have gone through their big reinvestment programme more of the cash flow will be coming through to investors. I wouldn't say that they are immune to the economic cycle, but they are pretty close to it. In 2008 they didn't see any fall in business. In fact, they got more because even if people's incomes were hit and they couldn't afford to go abroad, they still wanted somewhere pleasant to stay. The fund has returned about 10% per annum compounded since I bought it the first time, and I have been regularly adding to my holding for the last decade at least.

You should be aware that this fund, unlike all the others I own, is an unregulated fund, meaning there is less protection for you as an investor should anything go badly wrong. Because of its specialist nature, the fund has been closed to new investors for some time. You won't find it listed on any of the leading platforms for individual investors, and I therefore suggest that you don't waste time trying to find it.

Royal London Sterling Extra Yield

The last few years have been exceptional ones in the bond markets. Yields fell quite sharply after the financial crisis, but since then, despite most pundits expecting yields to start rising as economies started to recover (which normally happens after crises), they have instead carried on falling. They are now at the lowest levels that anyone still working can remember. You can lend money to the government for ten years and get a return of just 2% – historically a very poor reward for lending money to such profligate spenders!

There are several reason why bond yields have remained so low. One is that inflation has been falling; the Consumer Price Index is down from 5% a few years ago to less than 1% today. Another is that governments and central banks have deliberately been taking steps to keep interest rates as low as possible. With its quantitative easing policy, the Bank of England injected £375 billion of new money into the banking system in an effort to keep the economy moving. To do that it bought billions of pounds worth of government bonds. The Americans and Japanese have been doing the same thing.

On the plus side, low bond yields and unprecedented buying by central banks means that the price of government bonds has continued to rise. (Bond prices fall when yields decline, and vice versa.) That in turn has helped lift the price of all other kinds of fixed-interest investments, which traditionally are priced by reference to government bonds. That includes corporate bonds, which are effectively debt that has been issued by companies.

The Royal London fund is the main way that I have been gaining my exposure to the bond market. I have been fairly relaxed about the outlook for bonds for a few years now. Although valuations look very stretched on historic measures, my view has been that interest rates are going nowhere fast for some time. This is not a normal interest-rate cycle. With so much debt still overhanging the economy, the authorities are going to do everything they can to keep the cost of borrowing as low as possible for as long as they can. That reduces the risk of owning bonds, even at these fancy prices.

I will admit that I have still been surprised by quite how far bond prices have risen. The Royal London fund is very much at the riskier end of the bond spectrum, since it primarily invests in high-yield corporate bonds, and not just the ones with the best credit ratings. The fund suffered hugely during the financial crisis, when it lost at least 40% of its value, and that was when I started to put some money into it. The yield on the fund had reached more than 10% at one point, but since then it has made a good deal of money out of its high-yield bonds (an industry euphemism for what were once called junk bonds, but an often underrated asset class). The fund's capital value has risen by more than 150% over five years with income reinvested – not the kind of performance that you normally expect from a bond fund. If you take the income, it pays a tax-free yield of around 6%, with some handsome capital gains on top until the last couple of years.

Although many pundits have been worrying about what a period of soaring interest rates could do to the value of bonds, I don't believe that rates are going to rise by much (if at all) for quite some time. Financial crises take a long time to work their way through the system and we may be only halfway through the process of recovery after the big banking bust of 2008. As long as the risk of a large bond market sell-off remains remote, I will continue to keep some money in bonds for protection, even though the returns are unlikely to match those of the past two decades, and if there is a big sell-off at some point I would be looking to buy back in if prices fall too far.

Marlborough small-cap funds

Giles Hargreave has been one of the most successful UK small-cap fund managers for nearly 20 years. In recent years, with our help in some cases, he has expanded the range of funds he offers so that they now include funds covering every part of the market capitalisation range. One of the surprising things to first-time investors is how big some so-called small-cap companies can be. An established company like Majestic Wine, a popular choice for many investors, is valued in the stock market at more than £250 million. At the other end of the spectrum there are some genuine minnows, companies that are valued in the stock market at less than £5m. Yet both qualify as small-cap investments.

There is clearly a huge difference between investing in these two kinds of company. A very small company may be dynamic and entrepreneurial and well on its way towards becoming a household name of the future, like Majestic. Or it may be a start-up company that is struggling to survive and will in time fade away altogether. You need a lot of specialist expertise and experience to distinguish between the two and between the good and the bad in both spaces. That is what Giles and other successful small-cap fund managers, such as Dan Nickols at Old Mutual and Harry Nimmo of Standard Life, have consistently shown they are able to do.

It is true that small-cap shares have had an exceptionally golden patch since the turn of the century. Academic studies tell us that smaller company shares should outperform over time, precisely because they are riskier and less liquid than their bigger counterparts. The scale of that outperformance since 2000 has been striking, making me very glad that I have maintained my exposure to this sector.

A particular feature of the small-cap sector is that there are a surprising number of smaller companies that pay a healthy and rising dividend out of their cash flow. That has been a particularly rewarding area in which to invest and one that Giles has managed to exploit very successfully. All his funds are very broadly diversified, with more than a hundred holdings, and he has shown himself to be highly skilled at selling or cutting his winners at the right time (a skill I envy). He rarely has more than 3% of his funds in any one company, to avoid the risk of being derailed by a single investment blowing up in his face.

Artemis Strategic Assets

The Artemis Strategic Assets fund employs a 'go anywhere' approach, with the flexibility to invest in equities, bonds, cash, commodities and currencies. It can also use derivatives to take short positions in certain types of assets, which can magnify returns but also increases risk. That makes it different from most of the other funds I own. The fund is managed by William Littlewood, who made his name in the 1990s when he ran the Jupiter Income Fund with great success.

The fund has a twin objective – to achieve returns greater than the FTSE All-Share Index *and* cash deposits over three year periods. While the fund sits in the IMA Flexible sector, I prefer to think of it as a total return fund – one that is designed to do well in all kinds of market conditions. Since its launch in May 2009, the fund has performed better than cash, but lagged the FTSE All-Share Index. The main drag on performance to date has been Littlewood's bond investments, where he has taken a big bet on bond yields rising sharply.

The fund is positioned to benefit from the falling prices of Japanese, French, UK, Italian and, to a lesser extent, US government bonds. As I noted earlier, these bonds have generally performed well in recent years and this has therefore cost the fund quite dearly. If it wasn't for the short bond positions, the fund would have performed broadly in line with the FTSE All-Share since launch. Littlewood has not changed his view that government bond prices, particularly in Japan, have been driven artificially higher, partly thanks to the effects of quantitative easing.

While he can't predict with certainty the exact timing, he continues to believe prices will fall and is happy to maintain the positions. The view that quantitative easing has distorted financial markets and that the amount of global debt is unsustainable is also reflected elsewhere in the portfolio. Currency exposure is currently biased towards Asian nations which do not have the same issues with excessive debt as we do in the West. In contrast, Littlewood believes the euro, Japanese yen and sterling are set to weaken and has positioned the fund to benefit from devaluation in these currencies.

Finally, about a tenth of the fund is invested in commodities, predominantly precious metals. Gold is the most significant investment, accounting for over 7%. As the price has fallen from the high of almost $1,900 reached in September 2011, the fund has been increasing its exposure. Gold is considered a store of value that cannot be debased by printing or creating more. It is held partly to diversify the portfolio against risk associated with excessive global debt and equity market volatility.

I have been somewhat disappointed with the fund's performance, but am happy to stick with it, given how different it is to the other things I hold. The advantage of a diversified, multi-asset fund such as this is that different areas of the portfolio will perform well at different times. Since launch the fund has tended to hold its value pretty well when stock markets have fallen, but lag behind when markets have risen strongly. That makes it a potential capital shelter in tough markets and therefore suitable either for a more defensive portfolio, or – as in my case – as ballast in an otherwise fairly aggressively positioned pension fund. It is doing something different to the other funds, and my thinking is that it rarely makes sense to have all your holdings positioned in the same direction.

Woodford Equity Income

In my opinion Neil Woodford is the best fund manager currently working in the UK. He has been investing in out-of-favour companies, with robust earnings and strong cash flow, for over 25 years. What makes him stand out from the average run-of-the-mill fund manager is that he is prepared to stick his neck out and make high-conviction bets on the companies and sectors he believes in, while areas he doesn't like – which in recent years have included banks and big oil companies – he avoids completely.

I have been investing in Neil's funds for nearly 20 years and have never regretted it. It was big news when he left Invesco Perpetual, where he had worked for 25 years, in 2014, with the intention of starting his own fund management business. His first fund, the Woodford Equity Income fund, was launched in June 2014 and his second, an investment trust to invest in a range of quoted and unquoted start-up businesses, mainly specialising in science and technology, in 2015.

The two largest funds that Neil managed at Invesco Perpetual, both income funds, were so successful over the years that they led him to having more than £33 billion in aggregate to manage by the time he left the firm. That was comfortably more than any other UK equity fund manager[17] has ever had to look after,

---

17   Richard Woolnough, who manages fixed-income funds for M&G, now has £35 billion of client money in his funds.

and the surprise in some ways was that his performance never seemed to suffer as a result, contrary to the conventional industry wisdom that most funds can become too big to manage.

Although I had owned one of Neil's funds at Invesco Perpetual, I was more than happy to switch all my holding into his first new fund, the Woodford Equity Income fund. What I like about Neil's approach is his refusal to obsess over short-term performance or to tinker with his investments all the time, two of the afflictions that go a long way to explain why the majority of funds disappoint and fail to beat their relevant benchmarks.

One of the sectors Neil has been most positive on in recent years is healthcare and pharmaceuticals. At the time of writing, around a third of the portfolio is invested in this area, including in large companies such as AstraZeneca and GlaxoSmithKline. They are held both for their potential to pay attractive dividends and ability to discover new drugs, which could boost future profits. He has also been a big investor in the tobacco sector for many years. Imperial Tobacco and British American Tobacco both feature among his top ten investments. The fund yields around 4%.

While the majority of the fund is invested in larger companies, Neil has also demonstrated his commitment to long-term investing by holding a number of smaller companies that need funding to grow. He is particularly interested in the drugs and technology businesses that are spun out of ground-breaking university research labs. These companies are the main focus of his second fund, the Woodford Patient Capital investment trust, launched in April 2015.

RIT Capital Partners

RIT Capital Partners is an investment trust, rather than an open-ended fund. There is no equivalent unit trust or OEIC. RIT was set up by Lord (then plain Jacob) Rothschild in 1988, after he split from the famous family firm. Its investment trust has one of the best performance records of all investment trusts over that period. It is a multi-asset vehicle that is managed in the careful, relatively conservative way that you would expect from someone with Rothschild's wealth, wisdom and experience.

The portfolio is split between listed, unquoted and other types of asset. Specialist analysts and fund managers look after the different components, but Lord Rothschild himself takes an active role in overseeing the balance of the portfolio. As an investment trust, the price of the shares does not always trade in line with the net asset value. In fact, RIT usually trades at a small premium, but if you are patient you may be lucky enough to buy in when it is trading at a discount, as it does from time to time. (In 2014 I was able to take advantage of the shares drifting to a 10% discount to top up my holding.) The dividend yield hovers around 2%, so this is primarily a capital-growth fund.

I regard it as a core holding that offers both long-term growth and some measure of protection during market downturns. I don't own many investment trusts, but they are particularly valuable when they offer something that you cannot replicate so easily through an open-ended fund. They are also particularly suitable for managers pursuing a strategy of investing in relatively illiquid assets. Property investment trusts are a good example, and RIT another.

Lindsell Train Global Equity

Lindsell Train Global Equity is a highly concentrated fund run by Nick Train and Michael Lindsell, a management pair we as a firm rate highly. The duo adopts a unique investment approach which has led to a long history of outperformance. I believe Nick Train and Michael Lindsell are exceptional stock-pickers and I view owning this fund as an excellent way to access their best ideas. Their company, in which they continue to hold the majority of the shares, also manages standalone UK and Japanese funds, although there is considerable overlap in their holdings.

My analysis suggests that stock selection has been the key driver of their returns. The Global Equity Fund was launched in 2011 and performance has been helped by a healthy weighting to the consumer goods sector, one of the strongest performing sectors over recent years. As value investors, the fund managers have a relatively conservative investment approach, which tends to come into its own in falling markets. Historically, tough market conditions have been where they have tended to add the most value.

What I like about the Lindsell Train approach is that they very much aim to run their clients' money as they would run their own. They also adopt a long-term, low-turnover investment strategy, which my experience suggests is one of the keys to sustained strong performance. They particularly like companies with wonderful brands, franchises and unique market positions, which can reward investors handsomely over the long term. This is essentially the same approach as that favoured by the legendary American investor Warren Buffett.

The fund looks for conservatively financed companies that produce a high and stable return on capital, and with a higher-than-average operating margin. Out of the MSCI World universe of 1,700 companies, only 180 of them qualify on their criteria as great companies, and are mostly to be found in industries such as consumer goods, asset management, packaged foods and specialised finance. Nick likes to point out that people will probably still be drinking beer made by Heineken, one of his favourite companies, in 300 years' time. That is not something you can yet say about Facebook or in fact any of the relatively new technology companies. The fund itself has a highly concentrated portfolio of 25–30 stocks, a third of which come from Japan.

My ISA investments

The biggest investment in my ISA – around 40% – is made up of the shares I own in Hargreaves Lansdown. Next is the Woodford Patient Capital Trust, two Marlborough small-cap funds, then the M&G Optimal Income, Newton Asian Income and shares in Provident Financial. The HL shares have been gradually accumulated through the company's save-as-you-earn schemes and have since matured. This highlights two important points: (1) the value of regular savings, especially in schemes such as save-as-you-earn schemes, which allow you to accumulate shares in your company at attractive prices and in reality very little in the way of risk; and (2) using an ISA to shelter both capital gains and income really does work well over the years. If I had owned my HL shares outside an ISA wrapper, I would be facing a huge capital gains tax bill if I ever sold them.

Too many people dismiss the annual allowance for save-as-you-earn schemes as being too small. Yet, as this example shows, the cumulative effects of using it can be huge, especially if the shares rise strongly in the meantime. Have I too much in one company? The answer an academic would give you is yes, but my defence is that in this case it is a company I know a lot about!

After this, my next largest holding is Woodford Patient Capital Trust which I bought at the time of its flotation. Neil Woodford is a fund manager I have known for over 20 years, and his Equity Income fund is a big holding in my SIPP. He has always had a huge enthusiasm for early-stage companies that may be little known and need help in financing and long-term capital. It is an area in which surprisingly few fund managers participate. This fund has no obligation to pay out any income, which does not make it a natural fit with my general preference for income generation. However, I am hoping for some great long-term capital gains from this holding. As for the other largest holdings, the Marlborough small-cap funds and Newton Asian Income also feature in my SIPP, and the only other holding I would highlight is M&G Optimal Income. This is a popular strategic bond fund where the manager Richard Woolnough makes calls on the direction of interest rates, currencies and bond yields.

Recent changes to the portfolio

It is important not to weigh down your portfolio with the costs of excessive trading. My philosophy in any event is to buy and hold the majority of my fund holdings for the long term. Although there will be periods of disappointing performance from some of the funds I own, I take the view that the best fund managers, if you can find them, will always make back more in the future than anything they may lose in the short term. So I can afford to be reasonably phlegmatic about the need to make changes. Sticking with your favourite funds also reduces the impact of charges and trading costs on your fund's value.

There are exceptions to my general minimal changes rule, of course. When a fund manager like Neil Woodford leaves his current firm, although this does not often happen, I have few qualms about following them to another home. In other cases there may be cause for concern about a particular fund manager's form and appetite for the job, which justifies phasing out their funds from the portfolio. Although it is very well-paid, managing a fund is also a demanding job, as the pressure to perform can be intense.

The key question then is: has the fund manager still got the appetite for the hard work involved? Has he become the victim of his own success and perhaps begun to believe his own propaganda about how good he is? I can think of a couple of examples in the last few years that have prompted me to sell out of a fund completely on these sorts of grounds, but in general it is a rare occurrence – as indeed it should be if you have put the effort into doing your homework at the outset.

I am more inclined, as I mentioned before, to make more gradual shifts in the funds I own in my SIPP and ISA. This is typically done by using the income from existing holdings to build up positions in other funds that I either think have potential at the time, or which fit better with my changing objectives. So, with the need to generate income for retirement more in my mind now, I have been adding to my holdings in the HL Multi-Manager Income Growth Trust. I also added some more units in the Marlborough Multi-Cap Income Fund after a temporary dip in its performance. And I invested in Giles Hargreave's Marlborough Nano-Cap Growth Fund when it was launched.

Spending time on the portfolio

How much time should you spend looking over your portfolio and measuring its performance? That is a good question. Personally I don't spend a lot of time analysing the performance of my portfolio in great detail. That is partly because I live with the business every day of the week. Keeping an eye on the way the markets move, and seeing regular updates from my team on which funds are doing well, by now I have a pretty good feel for how well I am doing without having to measure it precisely. I know how much money I put in to my ISA and SIPP as the year goes by, so it is fairly easy, just by looking at the total value of each portfolio, and mentally deducting the amount I have put in, to get a rough idea of how well I am doing.

Another factor is that with a relatively mature pot of savings, I am now pretty well-diversified and I am not expecting spectacular gains from one year to the next. My primary aim is to generate future income, not to shoot the lights out with capital appreciation, happy though I am to take it when it occurs. I have already mentioned my regret at not cashing in on the gains that I did achieve for a while with specialist funds such as gold. Now I don't spend so much time looking for those kind of things. I am getting more risk-averse as I get older.

Nor do I spend much time thinking about what my target asset allocation should be, on the general principle that once you have decided on your broad asset-allocation framework, you should not spend a lot of time tinkering with it. These days, most good websites will have tools that enable you to drill down through your holdings to analyse what you own – and how well you have done – in huge detail. I certainly wouldn't want to stop you doing that once in a while, but I question how much added value you will get in return for the time it takes. The danger is that you end up with so much information that it paralyses you, stopping you from making any decisions.

Provided you are broadly happy with the overall mix of your portfolio, I prefer to focus more on the funds that I already own – are they doing what they promised to do? If so, I can't see the urgent need to change anything, unless they have become a disproportionately large part of what I have. What should I do with the income that they are producing? Are there new opportunities out there that I could be missing? The answer is of course that there are always tempting new opportunities to consider, but I simply caution that if you are happy with what you have, you don't need to be rushed into action.

My own bias has always been to stick with funds where the fund manager has a huge amount of experience and a proven track record over more than one economic and market cycle. I rarely invest in funds where the manager has less than a ten-year performance record for that reason (although that track record could have begun at another firm). While tomorrow's star fund managers will be starting out on their careers today, my experience is that it is rarely too late to catch them when they have proved themselves. The important thing is to be comfortable that you understand what the fund manager is trying to do, and have a high degree of conviction that he or she is the right person for your particular needs.

I don't spend a lot of time analysing the regional breakdown of the funds I own. The reason is that it matters very little these days where in the world a company is listed. Many companies whose shares are listed in the UK are multinational businesses whose revenues come from all over the globe. Only a tiny percentage of their business is actually done in the UK. Shell and Glaxo would be good examples. A fund that only picks shares from the FTSE 100 index, therefore, is not in reality investing only in the UK. (In a more extreme example, one of the companies in the S&P 500 index, the main measure of US stock market performance, does not do any business at all in the United States!)

It is true that the further down the size rankings you go in the UK stock market, the more UK-centric the companies tend to be. That is a factor to bear in mind, certainly. The good news is that there are a lot of very good UK companies at that level. However, some analysis we did recently at the firm showed that of all the main market indices around the world, the one that has most closely tracked the world index is the UK market. Even if you only held UK funds, in other words, you should expect pretty much the same outcome as you would get if you bought the world index, at least over the longer term.[18] To put this another way, there is a lot of correlation these days between many of the largest global stock markets, so if one suffers, so too in general do the others.

The same goes for the world's bond markets. In recent years, the trend in all the big developed markets, which includes the US, the UK, Europe and Japan, has been all one way – yields down, prices up. If I was being critical about the shape of my portfolio, I could say that I have not had enough exposure to the fixed-interest market in the last few years, when bonds of almost all kinds – government, corporate and junk – have all performed exceptionally well.

I have not been against the bond market in the last few years; I have been less worried about it than most commentators, mainly because even if interest rates do start to rise, I do not expect them to rise very far or very fast. But even though bonds have done well, my stock market investments have done even better. There may well come a time when bonds once more look more attractive and I will increase my exposure to them, but for now I am not holding my breath.

I can't emphasise enough when reviewing the progress of your portfolio the importance of being able to take a bird's eye view of everything that you own. Many investors have pots of money all over the place – a bit here, a bit there, some shares here, a fund or two there. That makes it much harder to keep track of

---

18   This has not been true of the last few years, however, when the UK market has tended to lag the world index. One reason is that the world index is dominated by the US stock market, which has performed much more strongly since the financial crisis than most other stock markets.

what is going on with your investments. It also creates a lot of extra work and headaches when it comes to filling in your tax return and keeping on top of any day-to-day decisions that need to be made. You will find it so much easier to monitor your holdings if you can consolidate most or all of your holdings onto a single platform. That way you can easily keep an eye on what is happening to all your investments. A good platform should also give you a complete record of all your transactions and a single consolidated tax certificate to add to your tax return.

Funds I have sold

It is rare for me to sell funds that I have held for a long time. Once you have decided that you have found a manager of real and rare talent, it makes no sense to jettison them without good reason. My holding period for funds typically runs to several years. When I do sell, it is as often as not because I have other portfolio considerations in mind, not because I have changed my mind about the quality of the fund or the talent of its manager. That said, there are occasions – for example, when a manger moves company or simply retires – when you have to say goodbye to an old favourite. Here are two examples of funds that I have recently sold.

Old Mutual UK Dynamic

The Old Mutual UK Dynamic fund was a favourite of mine for a long time. Old Mutual has historically specialised in small and mid-cap shares (although two years ago they recruited the outstanding large-cap specialist Richard Buxton from Schroders to round out their range). I have always thought that the Old Mutual team deserved to be running more money than they do, and as a firm we have been happy to back them from the beginning. This fund is run by a talented young fund manager called Luke Kerr.

Old Mutual's small and medium-sized companies research team is renowned for its high-quality research and stockpicking ability. What Luke Kerr does with the UK Dynamic fund now is blend the whole team's best ideas into a concentrated portfolio. He invests in companies of all sizes, with a tendency to increase exposure to larger companies when he is more cautious in his economic outlook. On the flipside, as his confidence grows, he will often increase exposure to higher-risk smaller and medium-sized companies. He runs a portfolio of around 80 stocks. I think the fund will do well, and Luke has the potential to become even better over the years. But for now, this fund no longer fits the bill for my needs and I sold it down as I started to build up the income component in my portfolio.

Schroder Absolute UK Dynamic

The Schroder Absolute UK Dynamic fund, as its name implies, is a so-called absolute return fund, one which rather like Artemis Strategic Assets aims to do well in all kinds of markets. For a number of years I used it to provide more ballast for my portfolio. It balanced some of the more aggressive equity-only funds I hold, and offered some protection against losing too much if and when the markets turned down. The fund was run by Paul Marriage, an experienced small-cap specialist, alongside another more traditional small company fund. It was rebranded as a Schroder fund after his former employer, Cazenove, was bought by Schroders a couple of years ago.

The fund focuses primarily on medium-sized and smaller companies, and is somewhat more aggressive than other absolute return funds, meaning that Paul is prepared to accept some modest short-term losses within the overall mandate of targeting a modest positive return in nearly all periods. Typically he will hold around 60% of the portfolio in companies that he particularly likes and the remainder will be short positions in companies that he thinks will fare relatively poorly, a strategy known in the industry as running a long-short portfolio).

The track record has been pretty good, unlike most funds in the absolute return sector, which have generally been very disappointing since they first appeared on the scene. (One fundamental reason may be that it is simply very difficult to do what they aim to do.) There have been periods when the fund has been closed to new investors. However, as with the Old Mutual fund, given my greater interest in finding new sources of income, it no longer features in my portfolio.

Points to remember

- Think of your SIPP, ISA and other holdings as one big portfolio.

- Your pension fund is really just another investment fund.

- You are likely to need more income as you near retirement. Income units and equity income are useful, flexible tools for that purpose.

- Put a maximum limit on how much you hold in any one fund.

- Avoid making too many decisions – try to keep it as simple as you can.

- If you find a good fund manager, it is a good idea to back him or her with a significant chunk of your money.

- Make sure you understand what a fund's philosophy is and whether it is in line with your objectives. That way you won't be surprised at how it behaves.

CHAPTER 8.
Other Ways to Invest

Passive investing

THERE IS NO DOUBT THAT SO-CALLED PASSIVE INVESTMENTS, in the form of index funds and exchange-traded funds (known as ETFs), have become a lot more popular in recent years. We can see that on the daily traffic on the Hargreaves Lansdown website, where we now publish regular research on both index funds and ETFs. (The key difference between the two is that the former can only be bought and sold once a day through the issuing company, while the latter can be bought and sold throughout the trading day in the stock market, just like shares.) The number of markets and sectors that are now covered by passive funds has grown enormously in the last 20 years, which if nothing else is good for choice.

While I don't own any myself, I would never say that passive funds are to be avoided. A broad market index fund can be a good starting point for a first-time investor looking to gain exposure to the UK or world stock markets. Until or unless you have confidence in your ability to pick the best actively managed funds, buying a plain vanilla tracker fund is the simplest and most efficient way to make a start as an investor. If you do buy an index, or tracker, fund, your first objective is to find a suitable index, such as the FTSE 100 or All-Share index. Next you need to make sure that the fund actually does what it say, namely track its benchmark index as closely as possible. Surprisingly, not all do that job that well. It can be an effort to find out what a fund's so-called 'tracking error' is, but it is an important piece of information. (Tracking error is measured as a percentage, and you are looking for a fund with a tracking error of less than 0.25%.) Index funds generally work best when tracking an index in the world's biggest, most liquid, stock markets.[19]

Assuming that they do the tracking part well, the objective then is to pick the funds that have the lowest charges, just as you would with any other commodity, which is what tracker funds essentially are. Costs are usually the biggest factor in determining tracker fund performance. Some of the core UK tracker funds we suggest, where HL is able to use its buying power to negotiate a particularly attractive price, have ongoing charges of less than one tenth of one per cent a year. For funds that track the main indices in big overseas markets, such as the S&P 500 index in the

---

19   The reason is that it is much easier for an index fund manager to replicate the shares that make up an index of large, well-known companies which are traded in large volumes every day than it is to track indices in smaller, less liquid stock markets.

United States, or the Nikkei or Topix indices in Japan, the charges are typically somewhat higher, but still reasonably competitive.

It is worth making the point that the more exotic the index being tracked, the higher the charges become and the more of a drag, invariably, those charges will impose on performance. The higher the charges, the more certain it is that those funds will fail to meet their own declared objective of matching the performance of the stock market they are seeking to replicate. Some of the earliest tracker funds that were launched in the UK back in the 1990s had shockingly high annual charges of 1% or more. If you do the maths, over a period of say ten years a fund with that level of charges is guaranteed to underperform its benchmark by a cumulative 15%, even if it tracks the index perfectly! That is money that comes straight out of your pocket and is a long way from being the market-matching return that you might have thought you were being promised.

One technique that tracker funds use to offset the adverse impact of their charges is a practice known as stock lending, where a fund lends its holdings to a third party in exchange for a modest fee. That brings in some useful revenue and helps to reduce the tracking error, but it also creates some additional risk. I would only recommend a fund that lends stock if the investors see the benefit in the form of lower fees and the risks are clearly disclosed and carefully managed. You need to make sure that you know whether your tracker fund is stock lending or not.

The argument for tracker funds is that they can be a reliable way to achieve better returns than the average fund in their sector. If the majority of actively managed funds underperform their benchmark, a tracker fund that actually does its job of replicating the performance of its index must, as a matter of definition, finish in the top half of the performance tables. If you are worried about the risks of losing money, that may be an important consideration. But if you think of fund performance being like football, even the most effective trackers will always be Championship rather than Premiership teams – decent, solid performers, but always in the second tier, not the first.

The question then is: why settle for second best if you can have the best? If you believe, as I do, that in-depth research and years of experience can help you identify the best funds in their sector, the case for picking actively managed funds is clear. Of course, actively managed funds do better in some markets than others – the US market has proved a particularly hard market for active managers to crack – but the only fundamental advantage of a tracker fund for most investors is that it eliminates specific fund manager risk. They can be a perfectly reasonable choice for investors who either prefer not to do their own research or don't feel qualified to assess fund manager risk. As they should always have cheaper running costs, you do at least have the certainty of knowing that you are getting what you pay for – something that by definition is never the case with actively managed funds.

It is worth pointing out that not all ETFs are quite as simple or useful as the conventional index-tracking funds of the kind that I have been describing. There are actively managed ETFs as well as passive ones. Some of the more esoteric ones may, for example, be offering you the chance to make a leveraged bet on commodities. They can be extremely dangerous instruments that can easily lose you most of your money if the markets they are following go the wrong way. So it is important when looking at the range of ETFs to make sure that they really are what you think they are. As a general rule ETFs are in practice mostly used by traders who are speculating rather than investing in the traditional sense of the word. You should leave that kind of thing to the professionals.

Investment trusts

I have not said a lot so far about investment trusts, although I do own one or two myself (as you will have seen in the chapter on my personal portfolio) and they are in some respects an ideal investment vehicle for the DIY investor. Many of the principles of investing I have discussed in relation to unit trusts and OEICs apply equally to investment trusts, but it is undeniable that they are slightly more complicated and harder to explain, which can be a deterrent. While I have tried to spare the reader too many definitions and explanations, as they can easily be found on the internet, you will have to excuse me for going into slightly more detail in this section.

How investment trusts differ from unit trusts is that they are (a) closed-ended and (b) trade on the stock exchange. This means that to start life they need to raise money through a public offering of shares (an IPO, in technical jargon) and this gives them a fixed amount of starting capital. Unlike unit trusts, which create or cancel units at will, they can't grow or reduce their assets anything like as easily as a unit trust can.[20] The net asset value

---

20   What they can do is issue more shares from time to time, either by buying them in and reissuing them, or making what is called a C share issue. It is still a more cumbersome process.

of an investment trust generally rises and falls in line with the market and the expertise of the fund manager. Consequently, whereas the price of a unit in an open-ended fund should nearly always track its net asset value very closely, this is not so with investment trusts, whose share price is influenced by supply and demand.

If the trust is in fashion, or performance is stonkingly good, the shares may stand at a premium to net asset value. If you buy shares in the trust in these circumstances, you will be paying more than its current assets are worth. If on the other hand demand is poor or non-existent, and performance has been indifferent or worse, the trust's shares may well slip to a discount. The share price will then stand below the net asset value of the trust; now when you buy the shares, you will be paying less than the underlying value of its assets.

Got that? I can assure you that it isn't as complicated as it sounds. In simple terms, buying shares in an investment trust when they are at a discount is broadly a good idea – akin to something being in the January sales. Buying at a premium, however, certainly if it is more than say 3% to 5%, is usually a poor idea in the long run. There are some nuances behind this simple formula however! It depends a lot on why the discount has come about. If it is because the fund manager is no good and the trust's performance reflects that, the case for buying is weak, even if the price is a bargain basement one. But if it is because the whole sector is unfashionable, unwanted and unloved, it can often be an indication of genuine value and you should investigate it as a potential buying opportunity. Even in the first case, it may be worth keeping an eye on the trust as the board of directors always have the power to change the fund manager for someone better. If this happens, you will tend to see the discount start to narrow, though rarely immediately, which may still give you time to get on board.

When a trust is trading at a very large premium, it may be because the fund manager is exceptionally good, or more often it is an indication that the sector the trust invests in has become highly fashionable and therefore at risk of a sudden or dramatic change in sentiment. When a trust is trading at a premium of over 10%, it strongly suggests to me that you should not be buying it. It really has to go some in order to justify that kind of fancy rating. Even top-quality fund managers can see shares in their trust go from a premium to a discount. In those cases, however, they can often go back to a premium again, so keeping a watching brief on the share price and discount can be worthwhile, since from time to time it can throw up attractive opportunities.

One of the best examples of that phenomenon over the last five years has to be the case of Fidelity China Special Situations, which nicely illustrates a number of issues I have already mentioned about the difference between good and bad funds. In this case the story includes one of the UK's best fund managers, a sector that has drifted dramatically in and out of favour, and the impact of huge media exposure. The trust was born when Anthony Bolton, who had successfully run unit and investment trusts for Fidelity for more than 25 years, decided after a brief retirement that he wanted to move to Hong Kong in order to run a China fund for his old firm. Given his track record and high profile in the industry, coupled with the popularity of China as an investment theme, the launch of his new investment trust attracted a record amount of money, more than £500 million.

Initially the fund performed well, and before long was trading at a premium of more than 15% to net asset value – a classic example of a warning bell sounding. What happened next was that the Chinese stock market started to perform less well, and a couple of Mr Bolton's core stock selections turned out badly (one of his companies being accused of fraudulent accounting practices). Given his high profile, these problems inevitably hit the headlines in a big way. The fund slipped from a premium to a discount and, worse still, the share price fell as far as 70p, well below the issue price of 100p. The media was full of stories that Mr Bolton was unable to transfer his skills from the UK to China. Some gave the impression that he was over the hill and had lost his way. Many private investors expressed their disappointment by selling their holdings at between 70p and 90p a share.

By the time Mr Bolton retired from running the fund in 2013, the media was still largely hostile, some going so far as to imply that his time at the helm had been a failure. Although performance had already improved, the shares at that point were still trading on a discount of 14% to net asset value. Yet as the following chart shows, the reality was that he had beaten the fund's Chinese benchmark while he was in charge, which hardly justifies being called a failure. More to the point, he had already laid the seeds of a high-return stock portfolio. Since then the portfolio has blossomed under Dale Nicholls, its new manager. The Chinese stock market then recovered strongly, with the result that five years after launch shares in the fund stood at around 170p, more than double its price at the earlier low point.

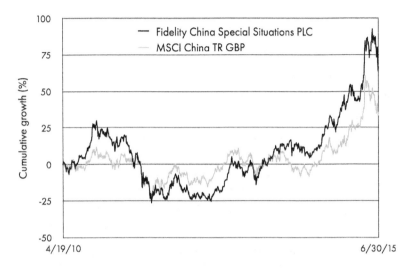

Figure 6.9: A matter of interpretation – the track record of the Fidelity China Special Situations fund.

Those who sold out after the initial disappointing performance missed out on a chance to make a 70% gain. This neatly illustrates the fact that you shouldn't believe everything you read in the media. A little time spent in research would have suggested that the move to a big discount was actually a classic buying opportunity, not a sell signal. Given that any equity investment should be seen as a long-term project, it was a mistake for investors to sell after just two years of experience, however disappointing the ride had been. The other point is that the Fidelity China Special Situations story illustrates how investing in investment trusts can be both more hazardous and more rewarding than investing in an equivalent unit trust, precisely because of the discount/premium cycle. It takes more work and more courage to invest this way – whether that is for you is a matter only you can decide.

Another important difference between investment trusts and unit trusts is that investment trusts can 'gear' their returns in a way that unit trusts cannot. What this means is that, if the board of directors agree, the trust can borrow money in order to boost the amount of capital that they have to invest. If the fund manager can make a greater return with this extra capital than it costs to borrow the money, the trust and its shareholders will be better off. (To continue the driving analogy, they have moved up a gear or two.) The scope for gearing is another factor that makes analysing investment trusts more complicated as the decision to gear or not can make a significant difference to investment performance. It also adds to the risk of share price volatility.

Each trust makes its own decision, adding to the diversity of returns. Some investment trusts never gear, believing that their portfolio is already risky enough. Gearing can work both ways. When interest rates were much higher than they are today, many trusts mistakenly geared up by borrowing at a fixed rate, in some cases locking into permanently high borrowing costs. With the march of time this problem has gradually unwound. In a world of very low interest rates, as we have today, gearing does appear to make more sense. The effect of gearing means that investment trusts in general outperform their unit trust equivalents when prices are rising in a bull market, but are certain to suffer disproportionately the next time the stock market takes a tumble. Care therefore needs to be taken when comparing unit trusts and investment trusts. In the main, the last few years have been good to investment trusts, as they have had the double benefit of narrowing discounts and gearing. It will not always be so.

Should you be put off by the greater complexity of investment trusts? I don't think so, although it does obviously depend on how much time for research you have at your disposal. Potentially investment trusts are a rich feeding ground for the self-directed investor. There are plenty of pricing anomalies you may be able to exploit. One reason is that professional investment institutions, which once were big buyers of investment trusts, have steadily divested their holdings over the years in favour of managing their investments directly. In a market dominated by individual investors, pricing anomalies do not always disappear as quickly as they would do in the professional institutional market.

In my view their complexity means that investment trusts will never be mass market investment vehicles in the same way as unit trusts were designed to be. That is actually a good thing. If they were to become more broadly owned, it would remove most of the advantages that private investors enjoy with them today. The very first investment trust, Foreign & Colonial, was formed as long ago as 1868. Despite its long illustrious history, after more than 150 years it is still only capitalised at £2.5 billion. By contrast, in the few months since Neil Woodford launched his most recent unit trust in 2015, it has already attracted more than £6 billion of investors' money. Now that is what I call a mass-market product – simple, easy-to-own and simple to monitor. Investment trusts will never be that, but they do have other advantages instead.

You will see in the media that financial firms are often criticised for not recommending investment trusts more frequently. There is a simple reason for this. Many investment trusts are quite small and that makes it difficult for firms with large numbers of execution-only clients to suggest them. The reason is that buying and selling shares in many investment trusts in size is difficult. The top 20 largest trusts rarely trade more than £2 million in a day. This won't matter to a DIY investor who is looking to buy or sell between £1,000 and £10,000 of trust shares, or to advisors who can spread client orders over a period of time. But for a firm like ours with thousands of clients, recommending an investment trust could suddenly swamp the market with buy orders, something that could never happen with a unit trust.

Just suppose we recommended an investment trust through our newsletter. What might happen? The market makers, the professional firms that take and implement buy and sell orders, would see the recommendation and mark up the price of the trust before the orders came through. Buy orders on any significant scale could not all be fulfilled, leaving clients frustrated. Worse still, the clients might want compensation for failing to have their orders fulfilled, particularly if that price continues to move up. If our advice was to sell, then the problem would be even more acute. This is why platforms offering execution-only services are wary of investment trusts and is why I also think they are generally unsuitable for the mass market.

That does not mean they might not be right for you. If you can get to grips with understanding how investment trusts work, they can be an attractive way to invest. They can still help you even if most of your money is going into open-ended funds. (As explained in the previous chapter, I own shares in RIT Capital, in part because there is no open-ended alternative.) The premium or discount at which investment trusts trade can also be extremely useful in seeing how investor sentiment is moving. It can be a good indicator of whether a particular sector or market is on the cheap or expensive side. If many more trusts are trading at premiums, it may be flagging up that we are near to a market top, while large discounts across a number of sectors suggest the opposite.

Venture capital trusts

Venture capital trusts are another sector in which I have been able to invest profitably in the last few years. What is a VCT? Well, as its name suggests, it is an investment trust that invests in venture capital – in other words, providing capital for new or established businesses that need cash to develop their business, and are typically either too immature or perceived as too risky to be able to borrow that money from a bank or other commercial lender. Anyone who has watched *Dragons' Den* will know how many would-be entrepreneurs find they need both finance and professional expertise to get their fledgling businesses off the ground. Since the financial crisis, banks have been cutting back on their lending to small and medium-sized businesses and venture capital investors have stepped in to help fill the gap. As an investor in a VCT you effectively get a return from both the lending and the equity investment that the manager of the trust has made.

Managing a VCT – picking the right businesses to back and helping them to grow – is a specialist form of investment management. Most of the firms which offer VCTs are small boutiques that are independent of the big fund management companies such as Fidelity and Aberdeen Asset Management. Nurturing new and growing businesses is an important function in any capitalist system and governments of all political persuasion have traditionally tried to encouraged it by offering tax breaks for those who invest in them.

When I started out in investment the main form of tax incentive was called the Business Expansion Scheme, and it wasn't frankly a great success. Many of the businesses that were backed under this heading were rubbish – more Del Boy than Google – and the charges were quite high. Since then things have evolved a fair bit and today VCTs have become a valuable source of finance for new companies as well as a useful additional home for any spare cash you are lucky enough to have as an investor.

That is because each VCT will invest in a diversified portfolio of companies, some of which will work out well and some will not. With luck the successes will more than outweigh the number that for whatever reason fail. Because they are young and risky, start-up businesses can grow very quickly if things work out and you only need a handful of those to produce overall gains in a diversified, professionally managed portfolio.

Admittedly VCTs are most suitable for those who are lucky enough to have already built up a sizeable amount of savings or are close to using up their lifetime pension limit. Because of the importance that the government attaches to venture capital, the tax breaks can be very valuable, especially for those looking to generate more income from their capital. The main benefit from investing in a VCT has been that your initial investment can be set against tax and will normally give you a tax rebate equivalent to 30% of the money that you have invested. Thereafter any dividends you receive are free of income tax and there will be no capital gains tax to pay when you sell them. The tax relief is withdrawn if you fail to hold the shares in the VCT for at least five years[21].

As with an ISA, another benefit of investing in VCTs is that you don't have to bother including the dividend payments on your annual tax return. The main attraction to me, apart from knowing that money I would otherwise pay in tax is going to help small businesses that the banks won't touch, is the tax-free income which I know I will need and appreciate when I am older. Assuming that the government does not change the rules about what qualifies for the favourable tax treatment, I expect to be adding to my VCT portfolio for the next few years. My main complaint about VCTs is that their fees can be quite high. Many also charge a performance fee in addition to their annual management fee, a practice which I have never liked.

It is important to remember that the tax breaks only kick in if you buy shares in an initial fundraising, not when you buy them in the secondary market. Because they are illiquid, the prices in the secondary market tend to be volatile. During the financial

---

21   This was the case at the time of writing. The tax arrangements surrounding VCTs will be changing following intervention by the European Union, which may reduce their attractiveness and the way the trusts operate – it is important to take advice or keep up to date with these rule changes before investing.

crisis, a lot of VCTs went to big discounts of 30, 40 or even 50%. As an existing investor, all you can do is sit through those episodes, but if you are on the ball it can sometimes be worth buying more in the secondary market at those heavily discounted prices. Although you don't qualify for the initial tax relief, you still get the tax-free dividends and the prospect of capital gains on top as the discounts reduce over time.

My VCT portfolio includes funds run by the likes of Northern Venture, Maven and Mobeus. Some VCTs are quite specialised and I prefer to stick with the generalist ones, rather than say the AIM VCTs which invest mainly in quoted stocks in the AIM market, where you always have the option to buy the unit trusts that do the same thing.

By the nature of the business the payouts from VCTs can be quite lumpy. If you are lucky and your VCT has a spectacular success, you may get a special dividend as well as regular interim payments. A good recent example was when Octopus sold its stake in Zoopla, the online estate agent portal it had funded. Because they are more risky, I take a long-term view of my VCT holdings, as you have to do. However, my experience is that VCTs are not as risky as some people seem to think. By and large they are fantastic dividend payers.

The main problem is that VCTs can be difficult to analyse; they are mostly run by teams, and telling the good ones from the bad is not easy. The liquidity can be poor, so selling at the price you want can be difficult. Many VCTs trade at a discount to their net asset value (and the rules and tax reliefs keep changing, which I am afraid is an occupational hazard). However, it seems to me, looking back over the 20 years or so that VCTs have been around, that half a dozen or so companies have emerged from the pack as the best of the breed and rather than trying to cherry-pick the best ones, I aim to hold a cross-section of the proven performers.

Buy-to-let is not all it is cracked up to be

Technically buy-to-let is outside the scope of this book. Yet property has become a near religion in the UK. For many it is the asset class that never fails and it is certainly true that property has turned out extremely well for many. But for me property has always been about a place to live rather than investment. I don't even think of it as an investment, at least not in the case of buy-to-let, which only really started being a private investor option in the mid 1990s. Buy-to-let is really a business venture, not an investment; the two are very different.

It would be silly of me to suggest that buy-to-let isn't something to look at. But you should go in with your eyes open. I notice, for example, that its fans tend to place its origins in 1996, which was right at the bottom of the then property cycle, and give all sorts of statistics to prove how well it has done against all other asset classes. It is perfectly true that it has done well since that date, but as I have said elsewhere in this book, be careful of statistics. Start the comparison from other dates in the past and the numbers can look very different.

Property for most is far better understood than the stock market. After all you can see it and touch it. It also appears to be less volatile – but be careful, shares are priced every second, and property only occasionally, so the rises and falls in price are far better disguised.

Buy-to-let is a business and you need to approach it as such. It is far more hands-on than an investment and is now beginning to attract more regulatory requirements. For example, 2015 saw the introduction of new requirements on landlords to obtain proof of identity and nationality from their tenants; failure to do so can incur fines of up to £3,000.

Other factors that are extremely important to take note of when weighing up whether to try your hand as a property landlord are the costs of maintenance, agents' fees and tenancy voids (the gaps that inevitably occur when one tenant leaves and another has yet to arrive). All these will reduce your income return. If you are also gearing up and using a mortgage to buy the property you want to let out, the mortgage payments also need to be taken into consideration. True, the interest payments can be set against tax, but I wonder how long that will last.

In my view buy-to-let is mainly a business to generate income, which is especially valuable today when interest rates are so low. The yield you receive as rental income is very important to making buy-to-let a success. Does a yield of 5% sound enough? That is a figure I often hear talked about on the radio when the subject of buy-to-let comes up, especially in the southeast of England, where capital appreciation has driven prices higher and yields correspondingly lower. It may seem to stack up well against your bank or building society account, but think carefully. My view is that as a buy-to-let investor you should be looking for yields closer to the 7% to 9% mark to make it a sensible business.

It is possible to find properties that you can rent out for that amount, but they are often found in areas far away from where you might live yourself. You are not likely to be buying the house next door. The buy-to-let business, like any other, involves looking for areas with the greatest potential for profit. It requires a huge amount of work to do this properly. Of course, it may be that you will benefit from capital appreciation when you come to sell your property and this will bail you out after a poor income return. This is undoubtedly one of the reasons, along with ultra-cheap mortgages, that so many people have rushed into buy-to-let in the past few years.

But in my view the capital value should be seen as potential icing on the cake, not least because realising it is an all or nothing event.[22] The income is what you should concentrate on. There is no certainty that the handsome capital gains of the past 20 years from housing will be repeated in the future. In fact they are highly unlikely to materialise on anything like the same scale. When interest rates start to rise, they will inevitably change the economics of buy-to-let for the worse. With so many young people feeling unhappy about being priced out of housing altogether, the friendly climate for buy-to-let landlords may well change.

The taxation rules that favour buy-to-let are also liable to change[23]. Property prices could easily fall, as they have done in the past. It would be very unwise to think that in a period of rising interest rates and falling house prices, buy-to-let landlords may not find

---

22   Unless you are dividing a house into flats, you cannot easily manage your capital by selling out in tranches – for example, to manage your tax liabilities – as you can with financial investments.

23   In 2015 the chancellor announced plans to restrict the amount of interest that buy-to-let landlords can claim against tax. The rules on allowable costs are also being changed.

themselves facing a very uncomfortable financial squeeze. That could be accentuated by the fact that many buy-to-let properties are financed with cheap mortgages. Over the longer term, this leverage does have the potential to magnify potential capital returns, but the flip side is that that can also work the other way round once interest rates start to rise – even if, as I expect, any such rises are gradual and spread over a number of years.

So I say use buy-to-let if you are happy for it to take the time and effort that is inevitable by doing the proper due diligence that you might do on any other kind of investment. Don't be seduced by headline yields and remember the cost of buying property is very high and this will normally wipe out your first year's income anyway. Remember too that buy-to-let increases your exposure to property if you already live in a house. Don't think that property never falls in price. It does. And don't forget the hassle involved in dealing with tenants, maintenance and all the records you need to keep in order to run a business. Me? I looked at buy-to-let once and decided that equity income gave me far more peace of mind for far less work!

Investing in shares directly

You will have noticed that the book contains very little about buying and selling shares directly. That is because in writing I have relied heavily on my own experience and with the exception of the shares I own in Hargreaves Lansdown, investing directly in equities has never really been a big part of my experience. This is not because I have anything against doing so. I know many people who have been very successful at it. It is mainly because if you are going to do it properly, it requires considerably more time and effort – and also different skills – than I have to offer. I genuinely doubt that most people are willing (or able) to give up that amount of time. But please don't let me put you off!

With more than 3,000 funds to choose from, not counting offshore funds, I feel that I have more than enough to do to keep on top of my fund research duties. While I enjoy investment, I don't personally wish to spend all my spare time poring over company reports. I much prefer funds, as they give me instant diversification and a far better spread of investments than I could achieve on my own by buying shares. Another factor is that my job requires me to invest money on a global scale, where stock-picking is even harder to do. I am also lucky to have daily access to fund managers whose ability to pick shares is far greater than mine could ever be. As the old saying goes, if you want a friend for life, go buy a dog. If you want to pick great stocks, go hire a fund manager to do it for you (just make sure they really are that good!).

I have owned shares from time to time, and like most people in the investment business I am quite happy to tell you about some of my greatest triumphs. Back in the year 2000 I did find a ten-bagger (shorthand for a share that makes you ten times your money) in the shape of a company called Cambridge Antibodies. For a while I thought I had found the secret of how to turn lead into gold. I quickly came down with a bump, however, when I lost virtually everything I had invested in another share, a company called Knowledge Management Software. At the time I thought it was on its way to incredible success. It turned out to be a turkey, or a zero-bagger, instead. Honesty compels me to tell you this.

More recently I have done pretty well with a company called Provident Financial, whose capital value has almost doubled in the past couple of years. It also pays a good dividend. Here at least is a business that I can understand. Whether you approve of it or not, money lending has been with us since the age of man and is likely to still be with us in the future. What I like about Provident Financial is that it is a straightforward business with little in the way of technology or biotechnology to understand. It is also a share that I reckon I could easily see myself holding for the long term, which suits my particular style of investing. It isn't sexy. It isn't going to make ten times my money in a year. But equally it is not likely to go bust. I very much subscribe to the view that the best way to get rich is slowly.

I also know that many of tomorrow's stock market stars are already out there somewhere in the AIM and smaller company sectors of the stock market. I am enough of a realist to know that, with my limited time and lack of relevant skills, the chances of my being able to spot them are very small. If you are tempted by investing in shares directly, my advice is to be realistic with yourself about what you can do and the time you can spend on it. Maybe you are an investment genius. Many ordinary investors thought they were just that during the internet bubble, until it all came tumbling down. If you enjoy researching individual shares and have the time and the inclination, by all means press on, but do please go in with your eyes wide open. It helps a lot if you have had relevant experience in business or financial analysis. My advice would be to limit your share dealing initially to no more than 10% of your overall portfolio, in order to find out whether you have the temperament and skills to do the job well. You certainly won't know how good you are until you have lived through at least one serious market correction and found out how you feel when all your shares have fallen by 25% or more. Only if you survive that will you know for sure that you have got what it takes.

I always note with interest which shares the clients of Hargreaves Lansdown have been buying and selling in the largest quantities. 60% of clients hold at least one AIM stock, meaning they have been tempted by the riskier end of the stock market spectrum. The most popular AIM shares at the time of writing have been Quindell, Sirius Minerals, Monitise, IGas Energy and Falkland Oil and Gas. Dig down further into this list, and it becomes apparent that these types of stock are rarely held for the long term. That suggests that those who buy them are really speculating, or having a punt, rather than what I would call investing. To make things worse, even though the stock market as a whole is up, most of these stocks have lost money. All this buying and selling costs money. None of these stocks fit readily into my criteria of good long-term businesses that pay a good dividend and are likely to be around in many years' time. It makes me wonder: are the buyers having a bit of fun, or do they seriously expect to make money from their share dealing? And that is why I prefer to stick with my funds – less exciting, certainly, but a safer and more suitable option for my way of thinking.

Points to remember

- Passive funds are useful low-cost starting points for first-time investors.

- Actively managed funds cost more, but will repay the effort if your fund choices are good.

- Investment trusts are a reasonable practical alternative to unit trusts and OEICs – more complicated to understand and often more volatile, but with compensating advantages.

- Venture capital trusts are a terrific potential source of tax-free dividends.

- Think very carefully before opting to go into the buy-to-let market: it is a business as well as an investment.

- Buying shares directly can pay off very nicely, but requires much more time and effort from investors.

CHAPTER 9.

Reflections on a Three-Decade Career

I F YOU HAVE BEEN AROUND THE INVESTMENT BUSINESS AS LONG as I have, it is impossible not to develop some strong opinions about the way that the industry has developed and is regarded in the wider world. In this chapter I offer some thoughts on the things that bug me, together with some further reflections on aspects of investing that I have only touched on earlier in the book. Feel free to disagree with me if you wish! As I have learnt over the course of the last 30 plus years, nobody can claim to be right about every aspect of investment. Experience is certainly the best instructor I have had.

On the perils of forecasting

There have been some dramatic stock market crashes in my time as a professional investor. The 1987 crash was a huge shock at the time. The internet bubble and subsequent bust was simply one of the craziest episodes in the whole of market history. The scale of the 2007–09 financial crisis, when stock markets fell by 50% for the second time in less than ten years, was also dramatic.

I would make an exception of the internet bubble, but it is fair to say that most stock market falls, including the biggest crashes, were not forecast by anybody. The 1987 crash was a seismic shock to the industry. Nobody had seen the markets fall so fast so quickly. You couldn't deal in some unit trusts for three or four days. They simply wouldn't answer the phone. That had never happened before and wouldn't be allowed today.

In the aftermath of that crash, they wheeled out market historians such as J.K. Galbraith and all sorts of others who could remember the 1929 stock market crash on Wall Street, saying it was the end of the world. When you're young and only a few years into your investment career, as I was, you think, "Well, these people ought to know what they're talking about." But of course I was wrong, as were all those doomsters who said that the 1987 crash would usher in a new global depression.

What you realise as you get older is that a lot of people who work professionally in the investment business don't actually have a clue what they're talking about – and the more expert they are, the worse they usually are. You can make a great career out of sounding good, even if your forecasts are almost totally useless. Most economists fall into that category. They get very well paid for being wrong almost all the time. There has never yet been an economic recession that has been predicted by the majority of economists. I find it incredible that they get away with it, but they do.

Mind you the fund industry can lose its marbles as well. In the 1980s and 1990s, many investment trusts borrowed money at absurdly high fixed interest rates. That cost their shareholders a huge amount of money. Equitable Life, the pensions and life assurance company, notoriously went out of business after promising its clients guaranteed annuity rates that it could not possibly afford to pay when interest rates began to fall dramatically.

If nothing else, these examples show that the idea that professional investors will always do better than private investors is complete rubbish. In my experience, the institutional and professional investor can be every bit as idiotic as any private investor, and sometimes even more stupid. I have seen too many examples in my time to think differently.

It also means that if you are in the business, it pays to be quite humble. You could always be wrong in the future. I am not clever enough to tell you where the stock market is going to go this year or next. It is easy to be a multi-billionaire with hindsight, but at the time things are never as obvious as they seem to be afterwards. The best you can do is take a long-term view and look out for prices or markets that have reached an extreme and bet that they won't persist for long.

Something like that happened when interest rates reached 15% during the early 1990s. You just knew that could not be sustainable. Yet I remember having a hell of a lot of trouble trying to persuade a client to buy a guaranteed income bond that paid out 13% a year and would also give his capital back at the end of the policy's life – just think what that would be worth today. He just thought interest rates would go on rising indefinitely, which is what people tend to do – they just extrapolate from recent experience.

A good recent example is the Japanese stock market, which from a long-term historical perspective has looked undervalued compared to most other leading country equity markets. But there are still hundreds of investors who find it impossible to invest in the country's stock market. Why? Because there have been so many false dawns before in Japan, and many investors still bear the scars of trying to get back in too early. London house prices are another example. People who say that prices will never come down again have short memories. We have had big setbacks in house prices at least three times in my career and at some point we will have another one, though don't ask me to tell you when.

Dealing with market crises

Psychologically, as human beings we have a much greater aversion to losses than we have positive feelings about gains. That's why I don't gamble. Horse-racing is like investment in that the outcome is rarely very satisfying. If you bet and you win, you are disappointed because you should have put more money on the winner and if it loses you aren't satisfied because you shouldn't have put any money on it at all! Investing can sometimes be a bit like that too. When you get a winner, you think why didn't I put more of my portfolio in that? And if it's not doing well, you think why did I ever put any money in it in the first place?

Investments are basically driven by greed and fear. If you are going to be fearful all the time, I repeat what I said earlier. Investment is supposed to improve the quality of your life, but if you worry about it every second, then it's not having that effect. It is certain that anyone investing will at some point have to deal with a crisis or a big market fall. There have been plenty of 5–10% corrections in the stock market over the last 20 years and quite a few scares which led to even worse outcomes.

Instant communications means market moves happen much more quickly, both up and down. I think it's important for investors to appreciate that, whatever they invest in and however good the fund manager is, the likelihood is that at some stage your portfolio is going to take a hit. You've got to think, "How will I feel then? If I invest £100,000 and find it's only worth £85,000 in a year's time, how am I going to feel about that?"

There is a useful test you can take. Whenever you buy an investment, you should try and work out the worst-case scenario. When you get a mortgage I always ask clients, "What happens if interest rates go up and you have to pay 5% instead of 3%? Have you worked out how much money that is and can you pay it?" If you can't, I question whether you should be having that size of mortgage, or even a house at all. It is surprising to me how many people don't seem to think this way when it is really no more than common sense.

The same goes for investment. You need to have realistic expectations and be mentally prepared for the times when things are not going well. If your expectations are not fulfilled, you will naturally be disappointed. If that happens, don't look at everybody else – think about yourself, about the investment itself and whether you are as genuinely long-term in your approach as you think. Rather than panic, I suggest you go fishing or take some time out rather than let your emotions get the better of you. It's never fun to see your investments go down. Nobody enjoys it. But it is a fact of life and you have to know how to deal with it when it happens.

The speediest fall I have seen was October 1987. Then it was a huge shock because people had never seen a market fall so quickly. Wall Street on that Monday night fell 25%! London, on the Monday, had already fallen just over 10%, and the following day it fell 11.5%. Since 2000 we've had two falls of 50% in ten years, which is unusual, but it does underline the volatility of economic and financial cycles.

That tells you that you need to look longer term and you do have to make sure that you have sufficient cash around you to give you that buffer before you invest in the first place. Just because something goes down doesn't mean that it's a bad investment. An awful lot of the time, although people say, "You guys always say that," we end up saying, "It's a buying opportunity". It might be trite, but 99% of the time it's also bloody true!

This must be the only industry in the world, where, if prices go down, people don't buy more, but less. If I said there was a 50% sale on at Harrods people would flock there. But in stock markets, people go the opposite way, become fearful and often don't do anything at all! That's the best time to be looking to buy, even if there is always a lot of luck involved. I get asked, especially when markets go down, "What should we do?" My answer is always the same. I just say, "Look, if you've already got a well-balanced portfolio, and if you've sorted out what you want to buy, then buy a chunk, say 10% or 20% on day one, leave it for a while, and if the market takes a fall, I'd definitely be putting some more money in."

There's psychological pressure for the DIY investor because, if your investment starts to go down, do you take a small loss or do you just ride it through? Back in 2008, funds like Old Mutual's Small Cap fund and First State Asian Pacific all took a huge hit. They were down 40% or 50%. The DIY investor tends to say, "Well, if I had sold it at the top, that would have been great." I say back at them, "Yes, but would you have bought the shares back at the bottom?" The news at the bottom is always worse than it is at the top. People too readily get into the doom and gloom and they don't buy back what they have sold and so they lose it. If you'd held on to the Old Mutual fund in 2008, it has since risen by over 250%. The First State fund is up by a similar amount.

This all comes back to my point about decisions: the fewer you make, the better – the trouble is, if you are a seller one day and a buyer the next, both decisions have got to be right, and usually one at least is wrong. That's enough to make you lose money. When markets are bad, I'm tempted to say the best thing is to turn off the news, don't keep looking at your portfolio and focus instead on the long term.

Market squalls will come, and there could be two or three in a year, or there could be nothing for a year or so, but it is a racing certainty that over your lifetime you are going to experience some tough times. But as a general rule, markets and economies most of the time plough the middle course. It's never as bad as you think, and it's never as good as you think either.

If the market falls and a fund manager like Anthony Bolton, Neil Woodford or Nigel Thomas does poorly, it does not mean that they have become bad fund managers overnight. In fact, they're the ones who thanks to experience will keep their nerve, which is what you need. What you don't want is someone suddenly going off-base because something's happened to the market and he's doing something he wouldn't normally do. That's normally a recipe for disaster.

We always want a reason for something, but sometimes there's just not a good reason. Back in the internet bubble, when the end came in early 2000, there was no single piece of news that suddenly said that this technology wasn't going to work. In fact, everything that was said about technology in 2000 and what it was going to do we're seeing happen now. We can see that clearly now, but tech stocks still fell like a stone back then. Like the railway and canal bubble they were wonderful for the economy in the long run because, although there was huge over-speculation and over-building, it's exactly what the country needed. You would never have got all the railways being built if everyone had sat down and thought about it.

The final point I would put on the table is there are periods when markets do become overvalued or undervalued. There may be some indicators that tell you that your return over the long-term is likely to be higher or lower as a result. The famous buying point for the Hong Kong stock market is a PE of 8; when the market falls that low, it is almost invariably a good time to buy. It's quite remarkable over the last 30 years that the market has bounced off that level so often. It is a good example of how, rather than trying to make macro market or economic judgements, it is better to hold on to your historical perspective on where markets are and take a line from that. An objective signal is always better than relying on a personal or emotional approach.

That is why many fund managers prefer to concentrate on valuations in their chosen sectors and stick to that method. A fund manager such as Mark Slater at Slater Investments uses a lot of ratios when screening stocks, but he doesn't do a lot of macro. Anthony Bolton never did a lot of macro, at least until later in his career. Giles Hargreave is the same. Of course, they may always have an opinion, but the question I like to ask fund managers is not what they think about the general economic climate but: "Are you still finding opportunities in the stock market today?"

If they can answer that question in the affirmative, that can be very helpful when trying to decide whether market valuations are too high or not. If they say no, it pays to be cautious yourself. You might think that their answer would always be "Yes", but my experience is that the best fund managers – the ones who have been around for a while and are honest with themselves – are also pretty honest about sharing their current opinions.

The pensions revolution

I would be much happier if the government stopped tinkering with the pensions regime in this country. Pensions are the second most important financial asset that most people have, after their homes, and the endless messing with the rules about what you can and cannot do does few of us any good. However the recent pensions freedom changes first announced by George Osborne in 2014, and taken further in the 2015 Budget, are potential game-changers which – if they are left alone by future governments – will have a profound impact on millions of people's future financial wellbeing. The chances are that if you are reading this book you may well be one of them; and even if you are not you will find a lot of people talking about the issue.

That is certainly a change from the past, when the word pension tended to make people's eyes glaze over and the subject was often seen as a quite distinct subject from investment. Yet, of course, as I have mentioned more than once already, in reality they are not. For this I blame the final-salary scheme so beloved of the public sector and until recently also popular in the private sector. In this type of scheme, the liability to pay you a pension rested entirely on your employer. As an employee, there was little need to know anything about investment. Your pension was just a function of your final salary and length of service with the company – typically around two thirds of your salary. That was enough to cover most of your daily needs, with any savings you had managed to build up as a bonus. There was no need to keep tabs on what was happening to the stock market. Someone else would take care of all that.

Today, the age of lifetime employment and the final-salary scheme are long gone, at least in the private sector, which is why nearly everyone now needs to understand the basics of pensions in a way that was unnecessary before. The old way lives on mainly in the public sector, where nearly all workers are still in final-salary schemes. The beneficiaries include politicians, so perhaps it is no coincidence that the constant meddling with pensions rarely affects them directly. If they had a private pension, I am confident that they would acquire much greater understanding of what impact the changes they approve are likely to have on you and me. I cannot think of a more important change than making them face the same practical problems that the rest of us now have to do.

What is fortunately also true is that private pensions are much better value than they were 30 years ago, in the days of sky-high charges and commissions. The big change is that the liability has passed from the employer to the employee and the self-employed. Given that your pension fund may well be worth more than your house, this has become a huge personal responsibility. How much pension you end up receiving will depend in no small measure on how you choose to invest it. It is no longer enough to rely on someone else to make decisions on your behalf. You either have to make them yourself or find someone qualified to help you make them. There has never been a more important time to educate yourself on the subject.

The issues can be quite complex, but the point I hope to impress on you is the need to start thinking about your pension fund as what it really is: just another investment fund. The better your fund is invested, the bigger the pension you will be able to draw from it when the time comes. On a day-to-day basis, a personal pension is merely a tax-efficient savings plan – no more, no less. So treat it as such, alongside your other investments. If your employer has a defined contribution scheme, and pays into it alongside you, don't just automatically take the default fund choice the scheme offers. Have a look at how your money is being invested and whether there are better alternatives. If you decide that picking funds as I have described in this book is a realistic option for you, apply the results to your pension as well. If you take advice, the more interest you take in what your advisor is proposing, the more likely you are to end up with a satisfactory outcome. My argument would be: you really can't afford not to get involved.

This is not the place to go into every aspect of the issues raised by the new pensions regime, not least because the new rules only came into effect in the course of writing this book (and there are more changes still to come). We will need to see how it settles down. In practice I view these changes, which you can find summarised on government and other websites, as a real mixed bag. On the one hand, the freedoms not to have to choose an annuity and to be able to pass on your pension savings tax-free to your spouse or dependants if you die before the age of 75 are genuinely positive and ground-breaking improvements. For those who have accumulated significant pension pots already, these changes could be particularly valuable.

On the other hand, the steady process by which successive budgets have reduced the lifetime allowance and annual limits on pension contribution tax relief are backward steps that limit how much value the other pension changes will have, especially for the younger generation.[24] I also share the concerns of those

---

24   In 2015 the lifetime limit was reduced to £1m, although those who have already accumulated larger pension savings won't be penalised retrospectively by losing their past tax relief.

who fear that people with limited experience or knowledge about pensions are at risk of making mistakes and falling prey to wrongful sales patter, bad advice or even fraud. (God knows the pensions industry has enough skeletons in its cupboard on the first two of those counts.) Whatever else you do, therefore, I urge you not to do anything in a hurry until you have really understood the changes that are being proposed.

One of the real problems with pensions which rarely gets mentioned is that, as it is with buying a house, there is a lot of luck involved. So much depends on when you happen to retire (and later also, for your heirs and dependants, when you happen to die). What is happening to interest rates at the time, and how the stock and bond markets are being valued at those moments, can make a huge difference to how well off you are in retirement. If you take your pension as an annuity, as people were forced to do until they introduced the drawdown system, the level of annuity rates can vary quite significantly from one year to the next.

My father-in-law was one of the lucky ones. He retired in 1994, just when there was a sudden sharp rise in annuity rates. It was a year when the Federal Reserve, the US central bank, raised rates unexpectedly, causing havoc in the bond market. Annuity rates are normally priced off the yields on government bonds, and gilts had their worst year for 36 years, yields soaring and prices falling. It was a shock to the market, but good news for my father-in-law. He retired just as annuity rates peaked. For his £300,000 accumulated pension pot, he got almost 10% a year for the rest of his life – a real bargain as interest rates and inflation both went down from there. Today he would be lucky to get 5% from an annuity. He would need £700,000 to have the same annual income.

If you have opted for drawdown instead, taking what you think you need and leaving the rest invested, the same lottery applies, depending on where the markets are when you start drawing down. If you started to draw down your pension at the end of 2007, it would have been horrendous, as the stock market promptly fell by 50% over the next 18 months. If you had started in March 2009, you would have been in clover, as the stock market is up more than 100% since then! As nobody can confidently predict exactly how the markets are going to behave over such a short period, there is no way round the problem of luck that I can see. You have no choice but to accept "the slings and arrows of outrageous fortune", as Hamlet says.

Two difficult issues

The problem of timing certainly complicates two of the most difficult issues posed in pensions planning: (1) deciding how much you need to guarantee an enjoyable and stress-free retirement and (2) the problem of whether to choose the annuity route or drawdown. The pension freedom legislation frees everyone from the need to take an annuity if they don't want to, which is intuitively very attractive. What people don't like about an annuity is the idea that the insurance company goes off with all your money when you die. You give the insurance company all your savings and if you die the next day, the company cops the lot and no one else gets any of your money. Of course, if you live longer than the actuaries expect, you benefit at somebody else's expense, but the unfairness of it still rankles with many people. It has got worse as annuity rates have continued to fall.

The trouble is that drawdown is much more appealing to people as an idea, but devilishly difficult to get right in practice. Having managed drawdown for one or two clients, I have hated every moment of it, if I am honest. It is very stressful, knowing that you are always having to take a view about the markets despite knowing that it is impossible to foretell what they are going to do from one year to the next! If the markets are about to fall by 50% over the next two years, as happened twice in the last 15 years, what are you meant to do? It is easy to decide with 100% hindsight, but something of a nightmare at the time.

This is therefore one of my biggest worries about the pensions legislation changes. If professionals like me cannot be sure what the best drawdown strategy to adopt is, is it reasonable to think that most ordinary investors can do any better? There has to be a fair chance that if they do choose to go down the drawdown route they will eventually run out of money, forcing them back onto reliance on the state. In practice, given that the majority of people have less than £30,000 in their pension pot, many will simply take the cash and spend it.

As it is, something like 80% of all people with pensions fail to take any professional advice before deciding what to do when they retire. When they opt for an annuity, the great majority simply take the deal offered by their insurance company, instead of shopping around, as they should. That must also cost them thousands of pounds. It does not suggest to me that they are crying out for the opportunity to make any more decisions! I don't know if anyone has ever studied this in any depth, but my gut feeling is that most of the time most people who have chosen drawdown in the last ten years will probably look back now and wish that they hadn't given up the annuity option. The only way most people will have benefited from going for drawdown is if they happen to die early – and that is not the kind of thing that you want to wish for – at least I don't!

To my mind, therefore drawdown only works for quite sophisticated people with a lot of money. Government claims that five-million existing annuity holders will benefit from the freedom to exchange their annuity for a cash sum needs to be put into context. It is not yet clear that such a scheme can be built and even if it is, it might only benefit a small minority. For most people, I venture to suggest that it will probably make sense to retain their existing secure annuity income. Anyone who does opt for drawdown should keep the equivalent of at least two years of pension income as a reserve, so that if the markets do tumble, you can stop the drawdown payments rather than see your capital diminish any further.

On the need to save

With pensions still in mind, I cannot reiterate enough times (a) how important it is to start saving early, and (b) why it is worth taking the trouble to read more about investment and – as more and more are doing – become something of a DIY investor yourself. I worry that most people are too put off or frightened about how complex it all seems to do that. If they need advice, they don't where or how to get it. There is a genuine problem in this country that most advisors won't touch you unless you have a minimum of £250,000 or so in assets.

If you haven't got that sort of money, or are only just starting out down that road, you really have no option but to try and fend a bit more for yourself. After all, if you never start investing, you may never get to the stage where you can afford good financial advice. Even then you may well want to go on taking an active interest. Why? Because what most financial advisors offer is actually not investment expertise itself, but financial planning.

Financial planning involves looking at your overall circumstances – whether you have a property, the age and needs of your children, life assurance, pensions and so on – as much as it does doing the actual investment of any money that you have. Of course, many financial planners would love you to hire them to look after their money on a discretionary basis, and earn another fee that way. Sadly many of them simply aren't that good at the investment part of the equation. You know the old saying: "If you want to make a small fortune, start with a big one". I am afraid that it is often true.

I like to contrast what happens in investment with the way people go about buying a car. You don't need to know how an internal combustion engine works to buy a car, yet when people do go and buy a new car they won't normally just go into a garage and say, "I'll buy that red one," and then two weeks later complain that what they've bought is a two-seater and they've got a family of six!

But that's what seems to happen in finance so often. Whether or not you have got an advisor, or are doing it yourself, people just don't forearm themselves with things to ask or any basic understanding of what they are trying to achieve. I don't think the financial industry helps itself in this respect. Like all industries, it has its own jargon and needlessly complicates things.

Attitudes to money have changed over the years. Once upon a time unit trusts were very much the poor man's way into equity. If you were at the golf club, you couldn't really talk about unit trusts as you could about how well or how badly your Shell shares had done in the previous week. There was an incredible snob value in having a stockbroker. It was also bizarrely thought that having your own stockbroker was the way to get the best professional advice. Unit trusts didn't fit that bill at all, although ironically, because of their favourable capital gains tax position, they suited higher net worth people far better than they realised.

A big change to people's attitudes came in 1966 when Barclaycard came out and brilliantly called their card a credit card rather than an HP card. Hire purchase was seen as very working class and my parents, for example, would never have borrowed money. Of course, this was before inflation started to take off and the cost of money got much higher, but my father thought that HP was a shocking working class habit (as well as an expensive one).

Barclaycard brilliantly broke that by calling it a credit card. I take the consumer society to have started pretty much from there. If you remember, in those days Barclays just mailed out their credit cards. You didn't apply for them – they actually mailed them out to you, and you got a card more or less automatically. The biggest change is that it's still very easy to get credit, but thanks to regulation, it's much harder to get anything on savings and advice into the public arena.

It has always struck me that it is remarkably easy to go into John Lewis and get five grand's worth of credit within two or three minutes, but if you came into Hargreaves Lansdown with £5,000 and said "help me", you'd be here half the day! That is because of all the forms that have to be filled in and the background research into your circumstances and attitude to risk which we are required to undertake before we can give you advice on anything.

If we are ever to develop a proper savings culture in this country, which we need if we are to invest in the future of our economy, we have got to make saving and investing easier and simpler. Education is obviously a big part of the answer, but there must be a better way to incentivise people to spend less time gambling and more time trying to put their money to work in more productive ways. The rules governing TV advertising would be a good place to start.

The trouble with banks

My first piece of advice to any would-be DIY investor would be: don't go near a bank for almost anything on the savings or investment side. Obviously you need a current account and banks may be able to offer you a decent mortgage deal, though these days it really pays to shop around before you commit. Yet their bank is the first place that many people go. I suppose that is because it seems the obvious place to start.

The trouble is that banking is not what it used to be. We all learnt that with the most recent financial crisis. Over the last 20 years banks have gradually changed from being guardians of people's money and financial interests to giant sales and gambling machines that see their customers only as the source of more product and trading profits, not as people they can – and should – be trying to help.

Anyone who has dealt with a bank on the retail side will have seen for themselves what a rip-off they can be. Partly that is because virtually all branch employees are now salesmen in disguise. I can still remember walking into the Lloyds Bank in Teddington years ago and being struck by the fact that the first thing I saw was a graph showing how many endowments they had managed to sell in the past week.

My grandfather was a bank manager at National Provincial before it was merged with the Westminster Bank to become NatWest. He was what you would call an old-fashioned bank manager. He knew a lot about South African gold shares and would buy them for his customers when he thought they were cheap. Can you imagine a bank manager doing that today? He'd be thrown out. Bank managers today no longer owe their careers to how well they treat the customers of their branch, but to how well they meet sales targets set by some manager at regional or head office.

The real rot with the banks set in when they allowed the retail banks – the ones that take your money as deposits on the high street and lend them out to businesses and individuals – to be taken over by profit-chasing investment banks. Nearly all the scandals we have seen in the last few years –mis-selling of pensions and insurance, interest rate and foreign exchange rigging and so on – have stemmed from that calamitous change in culture and behaviour.

Although there have been some tentative steps at reform in the last few years, it will take many more years to stamp out the bad habits and poor decision-making that has been allowed to creep into the way our banks do business. I wish I could say that we are through the worst, but in all honesty I find that hard to do. Don't trust them with your money!

Financial product advertising

For years the regulators have introduced ever tougher rules to clamp down on misleading sales and marketing practices by financial services companies. I have no problem with that. God knows there have been enough scandals over the years. When I started out one of the big talking points was the advertising done by a firm called Barlow Clowes. This was run by a man who filled the newspapers advertising a fund that invested in government bonds, yet magically promised investors a higher income return than government bonds themselves were generating.

Everyone in the business was left scratching their heads wondering how on earth that could be possible. My boss Kean Seagar, to his credit, was absolutely adamant that we should not let any clients anywhere near the Barlow Clowes fund. And that was very sensible; it turned out that Barlow Clowes was a simple fraud that enabled its founder to live a champagne lifestyle with money that flowed in from gullible investors. It was a classic example of the old adage that if something appears to be too good to be true, then it almost certainly is.

At that time there were no regulators around to stop the advertisements appearing and the newspapers, although they did do some simple checks, were happy to print the advertisements and take the revenue. A few years later the regulators had to step in again to introduce rules spelling out exactly how fund companies should present figures showing the performance of their funds. That was amply justified: we all know that there are "lies, damned lies and statistics" and some of the fund firms took the black art of misleading adverts to new heights.

What puzzles me today is the growing mismatch between standards applied to different industries. You cannot launch a fund or write a prospectus for a share that is being listed on the stock market for the first time without having to add pages and pages of small print detailing the risks. It is one reason why you will rarely see a TV advertisement for a fund, however reputable the fund management company offering it.

Yet switch on the television and what do you see instead? Adverts for ambulance-chasing lawyers and loan companies that charge you unbelievable interest rates and endless advertisements that beg you to start gambling on sporting events! The latter even offer you money to get started on the gambling habit. You could easily lose all your money, but that is given nothing like the same prominence as it would be if you were being offered a perfectly dull and sensible investment product that could make you money over the next few years.

The last thing I want is to see us go back to a world where financial products are sold by misleading promotions. Print and social media still carry plenty of ads. But in a TV-dominated age it is not a great surprise that the country's savings rate has been so weak in recent years. Credit was far too readily available before the financial crisis and now we have a problem where it is often next to impossible to sell perfectly sound savings products to those who need them most.

The lack of savings is not just a young person's problem. Those in their 40s and early 50s were traditionally people with money, but today many in that age group have not really saved anything. They might have a house, but a house is not a bank account, and it may or may not be useful later on – that's a different argument. Suffice it to say that I wouldn't want to be relying on selling a property for a pension.

Dealing with the financial press

Those of us who have been in the funds business for many years know how important the personal finance press is to the industry. Both my first boss, Kean Seagar, and later Peter Hargreaves, were quick to realise how helpful getting coverage in the newspapers could be to their businesses. They made a point of getting to know personal finance journalists well and being ready to offer a quote on any topical issue.

They also placed adverts in the financial pages offering information and advice on funds and produced free brochures on things like capital transfer tax, which the papers were happy to promote to their readers. In his autobiography, Peter says that the first time he realised he was going to be a millionaire was when he went to his front door and found a huge pile of letters from readers responding to his first unit trust advert in the newspaper. At that point he knew he was onto a winner with his new business.

Since then the symbiotic relationship between the financial press and the funds industry has continued to grow in both scale and scope. Every week you will see a lot of advertisements for funds in the financial pages of the national newspapers and in the main weekly magazines such as *Money Observer, Investors Chronicle* and *Money Week*. The pace tends to become especially frenetic towards the end of the tax year, when the press is busy advising readers to make sure they take advantage of their annual ISA allowance and pension contribution tax relief. The amount of advertising has mushroomed since I started.

Every week you will also read scores of quotes from leading broking and advisory firms in articles about funds, pensions, mortgages and so on. Needless to say, Hargreaves Lansdown is always prominent amongst those being quoted, and I plead guilty to being a regular commentator on such issues as the funds we like as a firm and the latest developments in the markets. Fortunately I greatly enjoy that part of the job and I like to count a number of personal finance journalists among my friends.

Nevertheless, as they would be the first to confirm, I also have some regular beefs about the way the financial press seems to operate. Actually I think it is very important to distinguish between the business and City pages of the newspapers and the personal finance pages, which are typically separate. The personal finance pages are often included as a supplement or distinct section of the main newspaper, reflecting their very different agenda and readership.

In practice it is usually the editor of the City and business pages who has ultimate responsibility for the money pages. I have often thought that it should be the other way round, as what the personal finance pages are writing about is usually far more directly relevant to readers than the general business and City pages. It is all very well taking about Vodafone's profits, but that is not what most affects most people. These days the personal finance pages cover a lot more topics than they used to do. It is not just about investment. It is also your energy bill, car insurance, bank accounts and so on.

Ian Cowie, formerly at the *Telegraph*, now a columnist at the *Sunday Times*, is one of the longest-serving personal finance journalists. He tells a great story about how when the problems at Equitable Life first started to appear, he tried in vain to get his City page colleagues to take an interest in the story. At first they just weren't interested. It was only when he mentioned that some of the paper's employee pensions were invested with Equitable Life that they suddenly sat up and took notice. It made the top of the front page the next day.

My feeling is that in the last few years, and particularly since the financial crisis, personal finance journalism has developed much more of an edge to it. There is more of an agenda than I would have said was the case before. Partly that must be because of the failings of the banks. What remains the case is that the media play an important part in shaping what people think and unfortunately not everything they go after is right. It is clearly a lot to ask the DIY investor to read as many of the financial pages as I do every week, but if you want to take investing seriously, I think you do need to read a lot to stay up to date. I would suggest starting with the *Daily Mail* on Wednesday and either the *Financial Times*, *Times* or *Telegraph* on Saturday. The Saturday issue of the *Independent* is obviously a must read.[25] So too is the *Sunday Times*. You might also want to look at one of the magazines regularly as well. After six months or so you should have a pretty good idea of what is going on.

What worries me is that newspapers are clearly now failing business models. The internet is chewing them up, and they are struggling to respond. News today is a straight commodity. You don't need a newspaper to see the news. In fact, it's out of date by the time you've got it. What newspapers should be good at is analysis, and I think that is what they should be spending more time on. I still don't think they do enough of that. The trouble is that with so much online content to provide, journalists write too much, which leaves them less time to do the heavy-duty analysis that you would hope to see.

And what they do write about, particularly in the City sections, is too much about general economics, and not enough financial specifics. They think that the macroeconomic situation is important, but I suspect it just turns a lot of readers off. Too many economic and financial commentators work on a diet of doom and gloom, which can sometimes be right, but more often than not fails to be justified by later events. One of the biggest problems

---

25   I write a regular column there on Saturdays.

is that much of the economic data that they have to analyse is unreliable and regularly revised later – as good a case of 'garbage in, garbage out' as you can find. More to the point, commentators are often good at identifying problems but not so good at coming up with practical solutions about what investors should do.

That is particularly true when it comes to thinking about the stock market, which operates on a completely different cycle to the economy. For the last six years, there have been pages and pages of negative comment about the state of the world, its over-indebtedness and the folly of quantitative easing and other monetary policy measures. Yet at the same time stock markets have been booming. Small and mid-cap shares rose by more than 200% in the six years after the low point in 2009. Shares have been the place to be, but few commentators have consistently said so.

With hindsight what most of the commentators should have been saying is, "Pile into the markets because you're being underwritten by the central banks!" But I can't remember many who said that. On the contrary, most of them four or five years ago were talking about the risk that we would be seeing hyper-inflation by now, which of course we haven't seen at all – in fact, quite the reverse. Everyone is now worrying about the risk of deflation. It shows again that using the macro picture to make sense of the markets is much harder than you might think.

QE may well cause a problem in the end, but as far as I can see, there is no inflation problem, mainly because the banks, certainly in Europe, and I would say in the UK too, are still struggling. That is what has really crimped the economy. The government wants them to lend money but (a) people don't want the money and (b) because of tougher capital ratios and so on, banks can't lend the money – in fact, they're calling loans in. In Japan it took them 20 years to sort out their bank problem because there were so many bad debts on the books. You have to get that sorted as quickly as possible and in Europe, unlike the US, they haven't done that at all, which is why I think the economy is working far better over there. Unravelling the consequences of the global financial crisis is going to take time. It may be that we are in what I call 'the long middle' of the current cycle. The media, rather like politicians, are not too good at being patient.

Pressures on personal finance

Obviously, there is some really good stuff online and in the media, and there are plenty of column inches about funds in particular. But I am not sure much of what is in the financial media is helpful to investors. I once complained about a certain columnist in one of the national papers who writes about his portfolio once a month. I analysed what he had been saying and found that his performance was really poor. Yet when I told the editor of the section that his columnist was talking rubbish and his performance was dismal, the answer was that it didn't matter because he was well-known and his column was entertaining. It is easy to forget that newspapers are in the business of selling too.

One problem is that young personal finance journalists are generally badly paid and lacking in experience. Many don't have enough money to have direct experience of the subject they are writing about. Until you have lost a quarter of your money in a stock market downturn, it makes it difficult to appreciate what that involves! I do think there is more of a negative edge to what they write now. Some of the criticism is clearly deserved, as the financial services industry has hardly covered itself in glory. What shows through to me a lot of the time, however, is the lack of in-depth research.

The numbers of journalists are falling all the time because of cost-cutting and they still have to produce something very quickly. I often hear them say, "I haven't got any time to research!" So instead they rely heavily on research done by third parties, much of it by people with a vested interest in a certain outcome. I wish journalists would check the data in 'research findings' a bit more thoroughly. I think investors need to be quite careful when reading this kind of story not to take it at face value.

There is also another problem that needs to be mentioned, which is that some newspapers themselves are slowly but steadily moving into the financial advice business themselves. By that I mean that they are increasingly producing supplements and online services whose content is effectively provided by financial services companies as partners of the newspapers. This is in addition to the revenue they generate from readers clicking through from online adverts. If you see something like, "*The Daily X* annuity service", for example, you can be certain that the information will come from a chosen business partner and have bypassed the editorial department. At least one newspaper hired as its partner a firm of advisors that was later fined by the Financial Services Authority for recommending dodgy funds and selling payment protection insurance!

The danger is that readers think that the newspapers have done a huge amount of research to discover the best people to work alongside, when you and I know that their commercial departments have simply gone out to find the best deal! I have also heard from freelancers that it is well-known that certain organisations can't be criticised because of their commercial relationship with the newspaper.

When it comes to the stock market, I have to admit that we have all played along over the years with the newspapers' stock picks and market-forecasting game. I don't want to sound whiter than white, but a few years ago I stopped us giving predictions on where the FTSE index would end the following year, or picking shares of the year. I admit that I had done this for 12 or 13 years. For my FTSE forecast I simply used to add 10% to the current level, on the basis that some years I would get it right, and other years I would look a complete prat. But I never took it very seriously. Then about five years ago I happened to be almost bang on right, and I got all these emails from clients congratulating me! I suddenly realised that they really thought this was a serious bit of analysis, and they might start to believe it was useful information, not just a bit of end-of-year entertainment. So we've stopped doing it.

I would also say that I don't think TV does finance very well. The markets are not a very visual subject, especially now that we have abandoned live trading on the stock exchange floor and TV has never really got to grips with personal finance at all. It ought to be a good subject for radio, however. Some of the programmes, like *Wake Up to Money* and the *Today* programme, can be very good.

The trouble is they're on at a ridiculously early hour in the morning, which limits the size of their audience. It is true that *Money Box* on Radio 4 has been running for years but my impression is that it devotes less time to investment than it once did.

I don't want to end my feelings about the financial media on a negative note. There are some excellent personal finance journalists and freelancers out there who do an absolute cracking job and are very conscientious. The reader problem pages in the daily newspapers do a great service in getting redress for hard-done-by savers. It is amazing – though also slightly shocking – how quickly the threat of media coverage can fix a problem with government and industry bureaucracy. That is a very useful role, although to the extent that it highlights the incompetence of many companies in the business, it doesn't help to get people saving, as I wish they would.

What do I read?

What do I read? The short answer is a lot, but then it's part of my job. I read all the major newspapers and magazines such as *Money Observer*. My personal favourite is *MoneyWeek*, despite it having what I consider to be too much of a diet of doom and gloom. It is always challenging and gives an excellent rundown of the week's financial news. It also has an excellent iPad version.

If you are new to investment, you should try and read as much as possible, but I would avoid most of the macroeconomic stuff, as much of it is scary and not very helpful (not least because the figures that grab the headlines are often revised as time passes, making the original figures redundant). The problem with media is that sensation sells papers. Headlines which say that everything is OK do not tend to get read!

The articles I would suggest you concentrate on are those written by investment fund managers themselves. They can help you build a picture of what is going on in the fund universe. Some fund managers provide regular video clips in which they talk about their views, something unheard of years ago. Seeing fund managers being interviewed is a good way to help you understand their overall philosophy and objectives.

The internet is now a huge source of everything you might need. It only takes a few seconds to get definitions of any jargon you might not understand. But there are also plenty of other sites to help you, among which I would highlight **boringmoney.co.uk**, **trustnet.co.uk**, **citywire.co.uk**, **cashquestions.com** and **fairerfinance.com**. You will discover your own favourites in due course. Whatever you might think of social media, I also think that Twitter is becoming a useful source of information, as many market commentators and writers can be followed there. Among my favourites are **@woodfordfunds**, **@merrynsw**, **@georgemagnus1**, **@nfergus** (that's historian Niall Ferguson), **@jdsview** and **@paullewismoney**.

CHAPTER 10.
Final Thoughts

These are my nine key takeaways for DIY investors:

- If in doubt, save and invest a little bit more – the rewards will pay you back for years.

- If you can't sleep at night, you are probably not investing the right way for your particular needs and temperament.

- Patience is probably the most important discipline you need as an investor, and the hardest to maintain, especially when media commentators are either deeply gloomy or exceedingly optimistic. Keeping your head in these circumstances is the most important requirement of all.

- Don't be afraid of your own judgement. One thing I have learnt is that there are many clever people out there, but being clever and having common sense don't always go together. Since the financial crisis of 2008 most clever people seem to have been spectacularly wrong about many things.

- You need to find your own way and style of investing. I can tell you the mistakes I have made and I hope you will learn from them, but you have to find out what works for you and what suits your temperament.

- If there is one rule for investment it is that there is always an exception to that rule.

- Try not to get trapped in your own personal history and experience. The low inflation of the 1950s and 1960s trapped many into thinking that gilts were a solid, safe investment. In the 1970s high inflation wiped those investments out. Then, just when everyone had come to despise them in the late 1970s, along came a 30-year bull market in bonds! Today the talk is all of deflation. Anyone born in the 1980s or later can only remember low inflation and interest rates that rarely change and never go up. Do not presume that this will continue indefinitely. It won't. If you can spot the inflection point you will make a lot of money.

- Always have an open mind and be ready to question the statistics and any research you see. I have discovered over the years that much of it is very poor and flawed.

- When buying a fund make sure you look under the bonnet to get an understanding of the philosophy and style of the fund manager. This will help you respond the right way when things go right or wrong. If you know why you will be more likely to buy or sell at the right time, which is all that investing is ultimately about.

ACKNOWLEDGEMENTS

I admit when Steve Eckett of Harriman House first emailed me asking me to consider writing a book on finance, I thought it might be a wind-up, something that some of my colleagues have been very good at doing in the past. But in talking to Steve I soon realised he was deadly serious. His argument was that there was very little written about DIY investing that was any good, and if anyone could fill that gap, he thought it would be me. Well, I agree about the first part at least. There is a gap...

When I mentioned Steve's idea to Ian Gorham, the chief executive of Hargreaves Lansdown, he responded very positively and after that the die was cast. Ian's unfailing support for the book also helped me at those times when I thought about giving up on the whole project. I admit to having been slow off the mark. I am used to writing short pieces of just a few hundred words. I write a column for the *Independent* newspaper every Saturday, but that is seldom longer than 600 words. A book is a very different animal, needing a thought-out structure as well as good content. So I am indebted to Jonathan Davis who came in to assist me, interpret my ramblings and put them into much better English. Both he and Steve Eckett have the patience of Job.

I need to go back in time as well, because this book could never have been written if Kean Seager had not offered me that first job at the front door of my mother's house. I will always be grateful for that first opportunity – something every young person needs to help them on the career ladder. His encouragement and advice in my early career was invaluable.

Some very special thanks need to go to Peter Hargreaves and Stephen Lansdown for the incredible support I have had at Hargreaves Lansdown. It was Peter who first rang me out of the blue in 1998 suggesting we had a chat and proposing I come to help him with fund selection and PR. Accepting the job at HL was undoubtedly the best decision I have ever made (with apologies to my wife). It has also given me the most fun of my working life. As Peter likes to say, you spend a third of your life asleep, a third at home and a third at work. If you can get the last two right, you have reached Nirvana.

While Stephen has stepped away from the business I still see him for a chat now and then and Peter as a major shareholder is still involved in the business, despite standing down as a director. Hargreaves Lansdown has an open-floor policy. There are no special offices for directors and Peter and I have always worked within a few yards of each other. We have never known each other's extension number. We just shout across a row of desks, often to the annoyance of my colleagues.

I am lucky to work with a fantastic team of 14 research and PR professionals whose talents and hard work I happily acknowledge. There are too many to mention by name, but suffice it to say they are all far brighter than me. I give a special mention to Lee Gardhouse, who manages HL's multi-manager funds. I knew him before joining Hargreaves Lansdown as a young whippersnapper and it has been a pleasure to watch him grow in stature and experience ever since. He has become an invaluable sounding board for my investment decisions, both personal and professional. Every DIY investor needs a Lee Gardhouse.

Finally I owe a huge thank-you to my wife Annette, whose unfailing support kept me going, especially through the hard times. When I was despondent at times, or if stock markets had taken a big tumble, her words should be remembered by all investors: "Stop worrying. You know it will all bounce back eventually. Just be patient." Very wise words.

APPENDICES

Useful websites

It is easy to be confused by the jargon and technical terms used in the fund industry. The fund industry's trade association has a particularly useful glossary of fund terms which you can find at: **www.theinvestmentassociation.org/all-about-investment/ glossary.html**

You might also find this **explanation of fund yields** from the Hargreaves Lansdown (**hl.co.uk**) website helpful: **tinyurl.com/ HLfundyields**

The websites listed below also have a lot of information about fund terms and industry trends:

Fund prices, ratings and news

- **trustnet.co.uk**
- **morningstar.co.uk**
- **citywire.co.uk**

- **iii.co.uk**

- **hl.co.uk**

Industry websites

- **theinvestmentassociation.org** (open-ended funds)

- **theaic.co.uk** (investment trusts and VCTs)

News

- **bloomberg.co.uk**

- **ft.com**

Useful publications

- *Money Observer*

- *MoneyWeek*

- *The Times* and *Sunday Times*

- *Financial Times*

Analysing a fund

Here are some examples of the kind of information that is available to investors when analysing funds, with my comments. The example I have used is the Artemis Income fund, which is mentioned in the text and is a fund that is rated highly by many professional investors and advisors.

The company's own factsheet

Income *Fund*

Performance (class R)

	Since launch*	5 years	3 years	1 year	6 months
Artemis Income	292.5%	75.1%	43.3%	5.8%	3.9%
FTSE All-Share TR	89.7%	66.6%	38.9%	2.6%	3.0%
FTSE 100 TR	87.5%	58.5%	30.4%	0.2%	1.4%
Sector average	123.2%	74.5%	46.4%	6.5%	5.0%
Position in sector	1/51	37/67	49/79	52/84	57/86
Quartile	1	3	3	3	3

Percentage growth 12 months to 30 June

2015	2014	2013	2012	2011
5.8%	11.5%	21.3%	2.5%	19.2%

Value of £1,000 invested at launch to 30 June 2015

Please remember that past performance is not a guide to the future. * Data from 8 June 2000. Source: Lipper Limited, distribution units, bid to bid in sterling with net income reinvested to 30 June 2015. All figures show total returns. Sector is IA UK Equity Income, universe of funds is those reporting net of UK taxes.

Current prices and yield

Bid price (dist units)	206.56p
Bid price (acc units)	346.14p
Offer price (dist units)	218.86p
Offer price (acc units)	366.76p
Historic yield (dist units)	3.9%
Historic yield (acc units)	3.6%

Investment information

Minimum lump sum investment	£1,000
Minimum monthly investment	£50
Initial charge	5.25%
Ongoing charge (dist units)	1.54%
Ongoing charge (acc units)	1.54%

The initial charge is currently waived. The ongoing charge includes the annual management charge of 1.5% and is shown as at the date of the Key investor information Document (KIID), where a full explanation of the fund's charges can be found.

Performance (class I)

	Since launch*	5 years	3 years	1 year	6 months
Artemis Income	39.6%	81.7%	45.6%	6.6%	4.3%
FTSE All-Share TR	58.9%	66.6%	38.9%	2.6%	3.0%
FTSE 100 TR	50.3%	58.5%	30.4%	0.2%	1.4%

Percentage growth 12 months to 30 June

2015	2014	2013	2012	2011
6.6%	12.5%	22.2%	3.3%	20.0%

Value of £1,000 invested at launch to 30 June 2015

Please remember that past performance is not a guide to the future. * Data from 7 March 2008. Source: Lipper Limited, distribution units, bid to bid in sterling with net income reinvested to 30 June 2015. All figures show total returns.

Current prices and yield

Bid price (dist units)	220.61p
Bid price (acc units)	368.13p
Offer price (dist units)	224.51p
Offer price (acc units)	371.25p
Historic yield (dist units)	3.9%
Historic yield (acc units)	3.6%

Investment information

Minimum lump sum investment	£250,000
Minimum monthly investment	n/a
Initial charge	1.00%
Ongoing charge (dist units)	0.79%
Ongoing charge (acc units)	0.79%

The initial charge is currently waived. The ongoing charge includes the annual management charge of 0.75% and is shown

My comments

All funds are required to produce monthly factsheets. They are the obvious starting point for your analysis. Note that there are two sections on the fund's performance. One (the class R units) goes back to the launch of the fund in June 2000. These are the units that ordinary individual investors can buy. The second (class I units) only goes back to 2008, and shows the performance of the institutional class, only available to professionals or investors with a minimum of £250,000 to invest.

The lower charges for bulk buyers explains why the performance has been better (81.7% over five years versus 75.1% for the retail class). It is also worth pointing out how the price of the accumulation units is significantly higher than that of the distribution (or income) units – 346p vs 206p for the bid price. This underlines how reinvesting the dividend from a fund, rather than taking it as income, will always produce a higher compounded return over time.

While the factsheet says that the fund has an initial charge of 5.25% and an annual management charge of 1.5%, in practice if you buy a fund through a broker, you will rarely have to pay the initial charge and since the rules on fund commissions were changed in 2013 the annual management charge will also be reduced by at least 0.75% provided you own the so-called unbundled units. So if you buy this fund through the HL platform, for example, the ongoing charge figure (OCF), the figure that combines the annual management charge with other costs charged by the fund, is now 0.70%.

Extracts from HL's research into a fund

My comments

This is an example of the kind of research about this fund that you will find on the HL platform. Other platforms will often have similar analysis, which goes beyond what the fund management company itself provides. The chart on this page, for example, traces the fund manager's performance not just back to the launch of the fund by Artemis in 2000, but further back in time to include his time with a previous employer, where he ran a similar equity income fund. We also comment on the fund's investment process and its contrarian investment style.

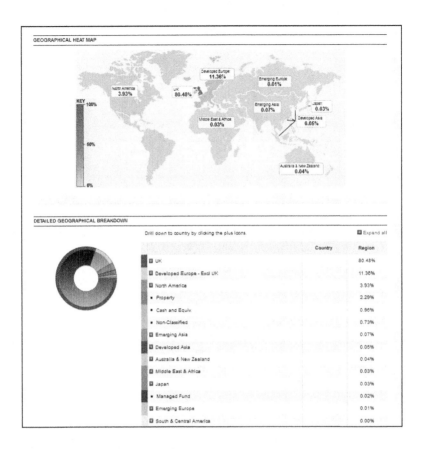

My comments

This graphic breaks down the regional balance of the fund's investments – not much value for a UK fund like this, but more useful with a global fund. It is worth noting that many of the company's largest investments are multinational companies, such as Shell and HSBC, which trade globally but happen to have their shares listed on the London stock exchange. If you measured where the companies owned by the fund generate their revenues, it would show a very different regional pattern.

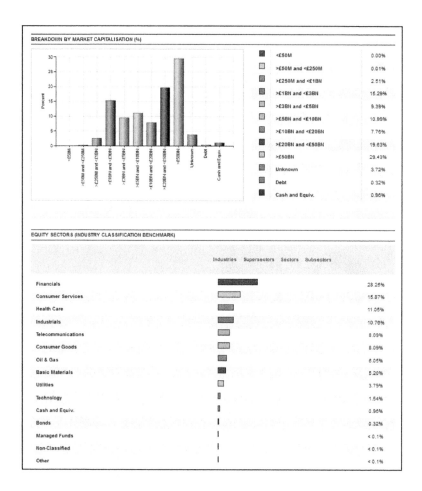

My comments

This analysis breaks down the sector and market capitalisation of the stocks that the fund owns. By comparing this to other funds, and with the main market indices, it generates valuable detail about the style of the fund. You can see that nearly 30% of the fund is invested in companies with a market value of more than £50 billion. It also has a large weighting in financial stocks. You can compare this to the makeup of the main London market indices (the FTSE 100 and FTSE All-Share Index) to see whether the fund manager has more in one sector than the market as a whole. Artemis Income is what the industry calls a large-cap fund.

Morningstar's verdict on this fund

The following is an example of the kind of factsheets about funds which you can obtain from independent analysis companies such as Morningstar. There is a lot of detail, and some of it may take some getting used to. I might draw your intention to the equity style map, which attempts to show how the fund stacks up against two main style measures – the size of the companies the fund invests in (large, medium or small) and the manager's general investment approach (growth, value or something in between). Being in the top left-hand quadrant indicates that Artemis Income is a large-cap value fund and that it has consistently followed this style over many years. The 'equity region exposure' graphic shows the result of the kind of look through geographic analysis I described earlier.

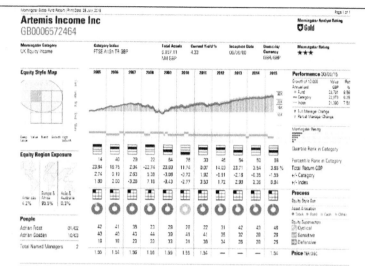

Artemis Income Inc
GB0006572464

Morningstar Analyst Rating
🛡 Gold

Morningstar Category	Category Index	Total Assets	Current Yield %	Inception Date	Domicile/Currency	Morningstar Rating
UK Equity Income	FTSE AllSh TR GBP	9,957.11 Mil GBP	4.33	06/06/00	GBR/GBP	★★★

This fund remains an outstanding choice in the UK equity-income sector.

Analyst View

Chetan Modi
Investment Research Analyst

Morningstar Analyst Rating	🛡 Gold
Morningstar Pillars	
Process	○ Positive
Performance	○ Positive
People	○ Positive
Parent	○ Positive
Price	◎ Neutral

Morningstar Analyst Rating
Morningstar evaluates mutual funds based on five pillars, which its analysts believe lead to funds that are more likely to outperform over the long term on a risk-adjusted basis.

Analyst Rating Spectrum
🛡 Gold 🛡 Silver 🛡 Bronze Neutral Negative

15 Apr, 2014 | This fund remains an outstanding choice in the UK equity-income sector.

The fund features a distinguished pairing in Adrian Frost and Adrian Gosden, who have worked together here since Oct 2003, although Frost took charge here in Jan 2002. The managers share an impressive amount of industry experience and also draw upon the expertise of their fellow Artemis managers. The resources have been bolstered since Nick Shenton joined in mid-2012 to provide dedicated analytical support.

The managers are disciplined in applying a process that is proven over the long term. They seek cash-generative companies by applying cash flow and dividend screens to their equity universe with the help of SmartGARP (Artemis' proprietary stock-screening model). They believe that focusing on free cash flow yield is the equivalent of valuing the company as if it were a bond. They subsequently compare the free cash flow yield with less risky rates of return—like money markets and bonds—and the focus on free cash flow gives greater flexibility than yield alone. There is

also a more qualitative element to their strategy in assessing management impact and their ability to allocate capital efficiently. Once the managers have narrowed their opportunity set, they focus on price/free cash flow as a valuation metric, taking into account both the level and direction of cash flow and its sustainability. We believe the strategy offers a well-thought-out process well-suited to primarily generating a desired income for investors.

Their flexible strategy has provided investors with strong returns and decent yields over the long term. Since the beginning of 2002 to the end of Feb 2014, the fund gained an annualised 9.07%. Those returns put the fund ahead of the average peer in the Morningstar UK Equity Income Category and the FTSE All-Share benchmark by 112 and 234 basis points per annum. We believe the pairing of experienced managers Frost and Gosden combined with their robust strategy gives the fund a strong chance of continuing its success. It retains its Gold rating.

Report as at 26 Jul 2015

Artemis Income Acc

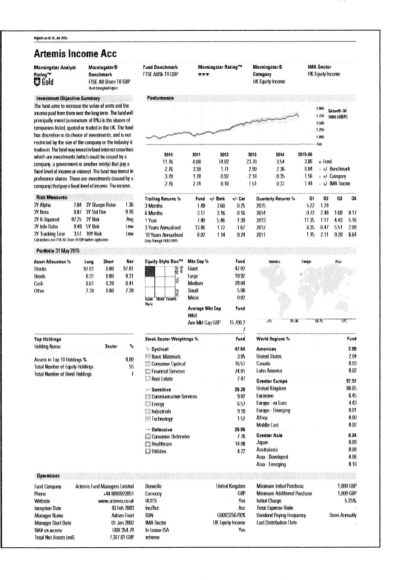

Morningstar Analyst Rating™	Morningstar® Benchmark	Fund Benchmark	Morningstar Rating™	Morningstar® Category	IMA Sector
🛡 Gold	FTSE All Share TR GBP (last sampled input)	FTSE AllSh TR GBP	★★★	UK Equity Income	UK Equity Income

Investment Objective Summary

The fund aims to increase the value of units and the income paid from them over the long term. The fund will principally invest (a minimum of 8%) in the shares of companies listed, quoted or traded in the UK. The fund has discretion in its choice of investments, and is not restricted by the size of the company or the industry it trades in. The fund may invest in fixed interest securities which are investments (which could be issued by a company, a government or another entity) that pay a fixed level of income or interest. The fund may invest in preference shares. These are investments (issued by a company) that pay a fixed level of income. The income...

Performance

	2010	2011	2012	2013	2014	2015-06	
	11.76	0.08	14.02	23.70	3.54	3.86	◆ Fund
	-2.76	3.38	1.71	2.90	2.36	0.84	+/- Benchmark
	3.70	1.78	-0.92	-2.18	-0.35	-1.56	+/- Category
	-2.76	2.74	0.18	1.51	0.37	1.44	+/- IMA Sector

Risk Measures

3Y Alpha	2.84	3Y Sharpe Ratio	1.30
3Y Beta	0.87	3Y Std Dev	9.16
3Y R-Squared	87.25	3Y Risk	Avg
3Y Info Ratio	0.49	5Y Risk	Low
3Y Tracking Error	3.51	10Y Risk	Low

Calculations use FTSE All Share TR GBP (index application)

Trailing Returns %

	Fund	+/- Bmk	+/- Cat
3 Months	-1.49	3.60	0.25
6 Months	3.17	3.16	-0.16
1 Year	7.80	5.46	-1.39
3 Years Annualised	13.45	1.77	-1.67
10 Years Annualised	8.02	1.14	0.24

Data through 26/07/2015

Quarterly Returns %

	Q1	Q2	Q3	Q4
2015	5.22	-1.29		
2014	0.72	2.48	1.68	0.17
2013	11.35	1.17	4.43	5.16
2012	6.35	-0.47	5.51	2.09
2011	1.15	2.11	-9.28	6.64

Portfolio 31 May 2015

Asset Allocation %

	Long	Short	Net
Stocks	97.01	0.00	97.01
Bonds	0.31	0.00	0.31
Cash	0.61	0.20	0.41
Other	2.28	0.00	2.28

Equity Style Box™

Value / Blend / Growth Style (Large / Mid / Small)

Mkt Cap %	Fund
Giant	47.02
Large	19.92
Medium	28.04
Small	5.00
Micro	0.02

Average Mkt Cap (Mil)	Fund
Avg Mkt Cap GBP	15,709.27

Top Holdings

Holding Name	Sector	%
Assets in Top 10 Holdings %		0.00
Total Number of Equity Holdings		55
Total Number of Bond Holdings		1

Stock Sector Weightings %

	Fund
⬡ Cyclical	47.84
🔹 Basic Materials	3.85
🔹 Consumer Cyclical	16.51
🔹 Financial Services	24.81
🔹 Real Estate	2.47
⬡ Sensitive	28.30
🔹 Communication Services	9.02
🔹 Energy	6.57
🔹 Industrials	9.19
🔹 Technology	1.52
⬡ Defensive	26.06
🔹 Consumer Defensive	7.76
🔹 Healthcare	14.08
🔹 Utilities	4.22

World Regions %

	Fund
Americas	2.09
United States	2.04
Canada	0.03
Latin America	0.02
Greater Europe	97.57
United Kingdom	86.05
Eurozone	6.45
Europe - ex Euro	4.43
Europe - Emerging	0.01
Africa	0.00
Middle East	0.02
Greater Asia	0.34
Japan	0.00
Australasia	0.09
Asia - Developed	0.06
Asia - Emerging	0.10

Operations

Fund Company	Artemis Fund Managers Limited	Domicile	United Kingdom
Phone	+44 8000922051	Currency	GBP
Website	www.artemis.co.uk	UCITS	Yes
Inception Date	03 Feb 2003	Inc/Acc	Acc
Manager Name	Adrian Frost	ISIN	GB0032567926
Manager Start Date	01 Jan 2002	IMA Sector	UK Equity Income
NAV 01 Jul 2015	GBX 354.70	In-house ISA scheme	Yes
Total Net Assets (mil)	7,307.61 GBP		

Minimum Initial Purchase	1,000 GBP
Minimum Additional Purchase	1,000 GBP
Initial Charge	5.25%
Total Expense Ratio	
Dividend Paying Frequency	Semi-Annually
Last Distribution Date	

Artemis Income Acc | ★★★ | 🛡Gold

Morningstar Rating™ (Relative to Category)			30/06/2015
	Morningstar Return	Morningstar Risk	Morningstar Rating™
3-Year	Below Average	Average	★★
5-Year	Below Average	Below Average	★★★
10-Year	Average	Below Average	★★★
Overall	Average	Below Average	★★★

Category : UK Equity Income   Click here to see our Methodology

Volatility Measurements			30/06/2015
3-Yr Std Dev	9.16 %	3-Yr Sharpe Ratio	1.30
3-Yr Mean Return	13.19 %		

Modern Portfolio Statistics	30/06/2015	30/06/2015
	Standard Index	Best Fit Index
	FTSE AllSh TR GBP	FTSE AllSh TR GBP
3-Yr R-Squared	87.25	87.25
3-Yr Beta	0.87	0.87
3-Yr Alpha	2.84	2.84

My comments

This page is definitely for those who are data freaks! Note that the risk (meaning the volatility of the fund's performance) has been below average over all but the most recent periods. Given that the long-run return has been average, the Sharpe ratio – a measure of risk-adjusted return – is positive at 1.30 (quite high by industry standards). The R-squared is an attempt to measure how closely the fund's holdings have performed compared to the UK market as a whole – broadly speaking, the closer to 100 the figure, the more closely the fund follows its benchmark. What this suggests is that the Artemis Income is a mainstream fund investing in the largest companies in the UK market and a solid performer that has added some value over and above what you might have obtained by buying a UK index tracker fund – but mainly because it has been less volatile rather than because of its exceptional returns. My analysis at HL would be slightly different to this conclusion – which underlines that even detailed statistical analysis will not always lead you to a clear-cut conclusion.

How multi-manager fund managers see Artemis Income

I suggested in the text that it might be useful to cross-check your analysis of a fund by seeing whether it features in the portfolios of the best multi-manager funds. Here is an extract from the most recent published portfolio of the Jupiter Merlin Income fund, one of the most popular multi-manager funds in the UK. You can see that Artemis Income is the third largest pure equity income fund, after Woodford Equity Income, Royal London Equity Income and M&G Global Dividend.

Top 10 Holdings			31/03/2015
			Portfolio
Total Number of Equity Holdings			0
Total Number of Bond Holdings			0
Assets in Top 10 Holdings			83.46
Name	Sector	Country	% of Assets
CF Woodford Equity Income Z GBP Inc		United Kingdom	12.80
GLG Strategic Bond D Inc		United Kingdom	10.48
M&G Global Dividend A Inc		United Kingdom	10.04
Royal London UK Equity Income Z GBP Inc		United Kingdom	9.29
IP UK Strategic Income Inc		United Kingdom	9.21
M&G Strategic Corporate Bond A Inc		United Kingdom	7.95
Jupiter UK Special Situations		United Kingdom	7.29
M&G Global Macro Bond A Inc		United Kingdom	5.67
Artemis Income Inc		United Kingdom	5.63
Jupiter Strategic Bond Inc		United Kingdom	5.11

You can also cross-check against the holdings of HL's Multi-Manager Income & Growth portfolio, where Artemis Income is the second largest holding after Woodford Equity Income. Given what I have already said about this fund, you probably won't be too surprised by this.

TOP 10 HOLDINGS	TOP 10 SECTORS	TOP 10 COUNTRIES

Security	Weight
Woodford CF Woodford Equity Income Class Z	18.58%
Artemis Income Class R	16.30%
Columbia Threadneedle Investments UK Equity Alpha Income	14.65%
J O Hambro CM UK Equity Income Class B	13.12%
Marlborough Multi Cap Income Class P	11.25%
Majedie UK Income Class X	7.97%
Jupiter Income Trust Class I	6.77%
Liontrust Macro Equity Income Class R	5.09%
First State Global Asian Equity Plus Class I	2.06%
Newton Global Income Shares	2.00%

INDEX

1970s economy 7
1987 stock market crash 114, 140, 195–7
2008 financial crisis
    banking 214
    forecasts 32–3, 109–10, 196
    fund investments 83–5
    lending rate 19
    portfolios 119
    venture capital trusts 183–6
    yields 150–1

A

Aberdeen Asset Management 184
absolute return funds 168–9
access issues 51–3, 61–3
accounting for investments 5
accumulation units 64, 144, 148, 235
actively managed fund investments 194
    costs 105–6
    exchange-traded funds 174–5
    patience 108–10
    selection issues 60–3, 70
addresses, internet 226, 232–3
administration advantages, websites
    51–4
adventurous portfolios 124
advertising 215–18, 223–4
aggregate dividend yield 64
AIM shares 192–3
AIM venture capital trusts 186
All-Share tracker funds 105
alternative investment methods 171–95
AMC *see* annual management charges
analysing fund investments 233–45

annual fees 47, 68–9, 104
annual investment income 63
annual management charges (AMC)
    68–9, 104
annual pension limits 206–7
annual percentage return rates 20
annuity 94, 197, 206–10, 223
Artemis Income Fund 73, 82–4, 93, 126,
    133, 148, 233–45
Artemis Strategic Assets 122–3, 126, 128,
    147, 154–6, 168
Artemis Strategic Bond 125–6, 154
articulation abilities 92
asset classes 18–38
asset return rates *see* return rates
asset-allocation 18–38, 112–38, 164
auto-enrolment pension schemes 3
average return rates 20, 25–7, 30, 34, 37

B

banks
    culture issues 213–15
    deposit return rates 19, 28, 36
    fund investments 56
Barclaycard 212–13
Barlow Clowes fund 215–16
bear markets 76, 83, 90–1, 109
benchmarks
    fund analysis 242–3
    fund investments 62–3, 122, 157,
        172–4, 178, 242–3
    investment trusts 178–9
    passive investments 174
    portfolios 122

benefits of
    fund investments 43–6
    taxes 2, 5, 27–9, 34, 38, 45–7, 51, 54,
        184–6
    websites 51–3
best for purpose funds 55–70
bias issues 49, 77, 81, 121–2
bird's eye views 166–7
BlackRock Gold & General Fund 134–5,
    145
blue chips 76–7
Bolton, Anthony 85, 177–80, 202–3
bonds (fixed-interest securities)
    basics of investing 18, 20, 24–5, 33–4,
        36–8
    fund investments 30, 58–60, 120, 156
    performance 150–2, 154–5, 166
    portfolios 116, 118–33, 138
    rates of return 18, 20, 24–5, 33–4,
        36–8
    yields 150–2, 154–5
'boutique' management companies 72–3
branded products 56–7
broad spread benefits 115
bucket viewpoints 24–5
Buffett, Warren 94, 137, 159
building and managing portfolios
    112–38
building society deposit return rates
    19–20, 23, 28
bull markets 78, 91, 180, 228
Business Expansion Scheme 184
business pages, press relationships 219
Buxton, Richard 167
buy-to-let property 5, 24, 187–90, 194

C

C share issue 175
calculating investment needs 15–16, 27,
    33–7, 39, 120, 122–3, 141

call-option strategies 94
Cambridge Antibodies 191
capital appreciation 63, 188–90
capital gains 2, 58–9, 63–5, 70
capital protection 58–9, 63–5, 70
capitalisation, fund analysis 238–9
caravan parks 149
career reflections 195–226
cash equivalents 59, 147, 149, 154
cash investments
    fund investments 59
    performance 147, 149, 154
    portfolios 119, 126–8, 137–8
    rates of return 18–26, 28–9, 31–2,
        34–8
cash reserves 24
categories, fund investments 57–60,
    65–70
character/personality considerations
    99–101
charges see costs
charts 51, 59, 80–91, 108, 110–11, 134–6,
    178–9, 236–7
Chatfeild-Roberts, John 99
children's portfolios 125
Chinese funds 85, 177–80
choice issues 5, 47, 56–66, 69–111
City pages, press relationships 219–21
classification
    fund investments 57–60, 65–70,
        75–6
    market sectors 64
closed-ended funds see investment trusts
commercial properties 20, 23
commission 48, 98
commodity products 118, 155
communications 81, 91–3, 199
compounding 20–3, 27, 34–5, 45–6
conservative portfolios 122–3
consistency, fund investments 68, 88,
    91–2, 107, 111

consumer price index (CPI) 17, 150
contribution calculations 15–16, 27, 33–7, 39, 120, 122–3, 141
convenience factors 43–4, 46, 54
conventional gilts 20, 23
corporate bonds 58–60, 118–19, 128, 151
correlations, portfolios 118–19
costs
    actively managed fund investments 105–6
    asset return rates 26–7, 29–30, 33, 36
    buy-to-let properties 188
    closed-ended funds 104
    financial advice 212–13
    financial plans 15
    fund investments 47–54, 62–3, 68–70, 101–6
    investment trusts 104
    mortgages 33
    open-ended funds 104
    passive investments 104, 172–3
    pension funds 141–2
    portfolios 132, 161–3
    venture capital trusts 185
    websites 51–2
    see also fees
Cowie, Ian 219
CPI *see* consumer price index
creating portfolios 5, 112–38
credit cards 212–13
criteria, fund classification 65–70
cruciality, flexible funds 143–6
Crux 73
culture issues, banks 213–15
currency considerations 62, 154–5

D

Daily Mail 220
Darwin Leisure 146, 148–50
data reliability 81–5, 111

dealing with losses 198–203
derivatives 94, 154
Deutsche Bank 99
direct share investments 190–4
disclaimers 140–2
disclosure standards 102
diversification
    fund investments 44–6
    investment trusts 180–1
    portfolios 117–27, 131–4
    return rates 30–2
    risk 117–27
dividends 153, 157–8, 192–4
    investment style 74
    percentage payments 64
    portfolios 133–5
    reinvesting 235
    small-cap funds 153
    taxes 7, 28, 139, 185–6
    venture capital trusts 185–6
division of financial assets 24–7
dollar premium 7
Dow Jones 77

E

earnings considerations 14
email alerts 93
endowments 9
Equitable Life 219
equities
    fund investments 58–60, 64–5, 67
    global equity funds 60, 73, 120, 123–5, 128, 147, 159–60
    portfolios 114, 119–20, 123–6, 129–32
    rates of return 18, 20, 23–6, 31–2, 34, 36–8
equity income funds 10
    basics of investing 18, 20, 23–6, 31–2, 34, 36–8

equity income funds *(cont)*
    performance 123–5, 128, 143–8, 154–7,
      159–61, 168–70
    portfolios 114, 120, 123, 126, 131–3
estate planning 15
European Union (EU) 185
eurozone 144
exchange-traded funds (ETF) 41–3, 61,
    171–5
expenditure considerations see costs
experience considerations
    fund investments 68, 73–4, 99, 111
    portfolios 163–5
    reflections on 195–226

F

factsheets 51, 92, 234–5, 239–42
Falkland Oil and Gas 193
family unit trusts 149
fashion
    investment styles 74–6
    portfolios 112–15, 138
fees
    buy-to-let properties 188
    fund investments 47, 51, 53–4, 68–9,
      101–6
    venture capital trusts 185
    see also costs
Fidelity China Special Situations 85,
    177–80
final-salary pension scheme 204–5
finance pressures, press relationships
    222–6
financial advice costs 212–13
financial asset division 24–7
financial crisis *see* 2008 financial crisis
financial plans
    basics 13–16, 38
    calculating investment needs 15–16
    costs 15

earnings 14
estate planning 15
how much you can invest 15–16
income 14
outgoings 15
pensions 211–13
financial press relationships 217–26
financial products
    advertising 215–17
    portfolios 128, 133–4
Financial Times 81, 95, 220
First State Asia Pacific Leaders 108–10,
    125, 128, 201
fixed income fund investments 30,
    58–60, 120, 156
fixed-interest securities, *see also* bonds
flexible funds 143–6
forecasting 32–3, 109–10, 195–8, 224
Foreign & Colonial Investment Trust
    funds 40, 181
Frost, Adrian 82–3
FTSE 100 index
    fund investments 61, 77, 90, 165, 239
    passive investing 172
    portfolios 118
    press relationships 224
FTSE All-Share Index
    Artemis Strategic Assets 154
    fund investments 61, 64, 77, 90–1,
      118, 154, 172, 239
    passive investing 172
    portfolios 136
    press relationships 224
fund analysis 233–45
fund companies, fund investments
    72–81, 85–95, 98–108
fund investments
    2008 financial crisis 83–5
    accumulation units 64, 148, 235
    active management 60–3
    advantages 43–6

fund investments *(cont)*
    analysis 233–45
    annual management charges 68–9, 104
    author's investment 139–70
    banks 56
    bear markets 76, 83, 90–1, 109
    benchmarks 62–3, 122, 157, 172–4, 178, 242–3
    benefits of 43–6
    best for purpose 55–70
    bias issues 49, 77, 81
    blue chips 76–7
    bonds 30, 58–60, 120, 156
    'boutique' management companies 72–3
    branded products 56–7
    call-option strategies 94
    capital gains 58–9, 63–5, 70
    capital protection 58–9, 63–5, 70
    cash/cash equivalents 59
    categories 57–60, 65–70
    character/personality considerations 99–101
    charts 51, 59, 80–91, 108, 110–11, 134–6, 178–9, 236–7
    choice issues 5, 47, 56–66, 69–111
    classification 57–60, 65–70, 75–6
    commission 48, 98
    communication skills 81, 91–3
    compounding 45–6
    consistency 68, 88, 91–2, 107, 111
    convenience 43–4, 46, 54
    corporate bonds 58–60, 119, 128, 151
    costs 47–54, 62–3, 68–70, 101–6
    data reliability 81–5, 111
    derivatives 94, 154
    disadvantages 46–50
    diversification 44–6
    dividends 153, 157–8, 192–4
        investment style 74

    percentage payments 64
    portfolios 133–5
    reinvesting 235
    small-cap funds 153
    taxes 7, 28, 139, 185–6
    venture capital trusts 185–6
email alerts 93
equities 58–60, 64–5, 67
experience considerations 68, 73–4, 99, 111
fees 47, 51, 53–4, 68–9, 101–6
Financial Times 81, 95, 220
fixed income 30, 58–60, 120, 156
fixed-interest securities 30, 58–60, 120, 156
FTSE 100 index 61, 77, 90, 118, 165, 172, 224, 239
FTSE All-Share Index 61, 64, 77, 90–1, 118, 154, 172, 239
fund companies 72–81, 85–95, 98–108
gilts/government bonds 60, 116–19, 207, 228
GLG Japan CoreAlpha Retail Acc A GBP 87–8
growth 58–9, 64, 67, 69, 74–6
hedging currency exposure 94
high street retailers 56
history 40–3
income 30, 58–60, 63–5, 70, 120, 156
Individual Savings Account 45–7, 51, 99
internet *see* websites
Invesco Perpetual High Income 89–90
Investment Association 57–60
investment styles 62, 67–8, 74–6, 80, 90–1, 111, 237
Japanese funds 87–8
large-cap companies 76, 90, 167, 239
management 60–3, 66–70

fund investments *(cont)*
  management *(cont)*
    character/personality
      considerations 99–101
    companies 72–81, 85–95, 98–108
    costs 101–6
  mergers 80
  mixed-asset income 58–9
  Morningstar website 75, 81, 92, 95,
    239–42
  nano-caps 107, 147, 163
  narrowing fields 55–70
  newspapers 80–1, 85, 95, 218–20,
    222–9
  number reliability 81–5, 111
  offshore/oversea funds 56, 59, 191
  on-line platforms *see* websites
  ongoing charges figure 69, 103–6
  past-performance 49, 66, 78–81,
    96–7
  patience 107–10
  pensions 46, 99, 205–8
  percentage rate fees 103
  performance 49, 66–9, 74–91, 96–7,
    100–11, 139–70
  personal pensions 58
  personality considerations 99–101
  pharmaceuticals 61, 114, 157
  portfolios 112–38
  problems with 46–50
  professional skill access 61–3
  professional viewpoints 81, 95–7
  property 58–60
  quantitative analysis 81, 83–5
  regulators 48, 66, 78, 85, 98, 102–3,
    141–2
  reports 78, 81, 85, 93, 97, 102
  research considerations 71–111,
    236–45
  Retail Distribution Review 97–8
  return rates 58–9, 63–5, 70, 80

risk factors 67, 80–1, 102
scale 44–5
selection issues 5, 47, 56–66, 69–111
selling 167–9
shares 41–5, 51, 58–62, 64–5, 67
Sharpe ratio 96, 242
simplicity benefits 91–3
small-cap shares 76–7, 90, 107, 111,
  125, 152–3, 160–1, 168, 201
specialist products 56, 58–60, 76, 95,
  111, 114, 128, 134–8, 145–6, 150, 163,
  184–7
star rating systems 95–6
sterling funds 60, 65, 150–2, 155
'stick to the discipline' 93–5
styles of investing 62, 67–8, 74–6,
  80, 90–1, 111, 237
tag confusion 65
tax benefits 45–7, 51, 54
technology products 58–9, 131–2
telecommunication products 58–9,
  61, 131
time considerations 49–50
trade associations 57–60
traps 49–50, 54
Trustnet website 81, 92, 95, 226
UK listed products 56, 58–67
Unicorn Income 89–90
value investing 74–6
volatility 80, 86, 95–6, 111
websites 50–4, 59–60
  alternative investments 175, 192
  charts 80–1, 86
  financial press relations 220, 226
  forecasting 195–6
  fund selection 80–1, 86, 95, 101
  investment trusts 175
  market crisis 202
  Morningstar 75, 81, 92, 95,
    239–42
  portfolios 114, 131

fund investments *(cont)*
   websites *(cont)*
      research 3, 92, 95
      why invest? 40–6
   see also passive investments
fund numbers, portfolios 127–33
Funds Library 81
future inflation rate scenarios 16–18

G

Gardhouse, Lee 81, 99, 140, 148
gas resources 136, 193
gearing 180–1
gilts (government bonds)
   fund investments 60, 116–19, 207, 228
   performance 150–1, 154
   portfolios 116–19
   rates of return 20, 23, 25–6, 31–2
   risk 116–19
   yields 150–1, 154
GLG Japan CoreAlpha Retail Acc A GBP 87–8
global equity funds 60, 73, 120, 123–5, 128, 147, 159–60
gold 134–5, 145, 155
government bonds *see* gilts
government debt 116, 119
Graham, Ben 10
growth, fund investments 58–9, 64, 67, 69, 74–6
guaranteed income bonds 197–8

H

Hargreave, Giles 76, 147, 152–3, 163, 203
Hargreave Hale 147
healthcare products 128, 157
hedge funds/hedging 94, 118
high street retailers 56
high-risk investments 116–18, 124–6

high-yield bonds 119, 133
hire purchase cards 212–13
historical overviews 40–3
HL fund investments 9–10, 57, 82, 92, 97–9, 122, 160–3, 172, 230–2, 235–6, 243–4
HL Multi-Manager Income & Growth Trust 125–6, 144, 146, 148, 163
HL shares 160–1
HL Wealth 150 list 97, 99
home ownership 24–5
Hong Kong 85, 177, 202–3
how much you can invest? 15–16

I

IGas Energy 193
importance of avoiding taxes 27–9
income
   buy-to-let properties 188–90
   financial plans 14
   fund investments 30, 58–60, 63–5, 70, 120, 156
   portfolios 114, 120–8, 131–3
   unit flexibility 144
Independent 220, 229
index funds 171–5
index-linked gilts 20, 23, 26
Individual Savings Accounts (ISA) 2, 27–9, 34, 38
   fund investments 45–7, 51, 99
   HL shares 160–1
   M&G Optimal Income 160–1
   Marlborough small-cap shares 160–1
   Newton Asian Income 160–1
   performance 139, 142–3, 146, 160–3, 170
   Provident Financial shares 160–1
   shares 160–1
   small-cap shares 160–1
   venture capital trusts 185
   websites 51

Individual Savings Accounts (ISA) *(cont)*
  Woodford Patient Capital Trust
    160–1
industry standards 102
inflation rates
  bond yields 150
  compounding effects 22–3
  future scenarios 16–18
  return rates 19–26, 30, 34, 38
  runaway scenarios 7, 18
information ratio 96
interest rates
  bond yields 152
  forecasting 197–8
  investment trusts 180–1
  market crisis 198–203
  rates of return 19, 25, 28, 31, 33, 36
internet
  bubble 192, 195–6, 202
  fund investments 50–4, 59–60
    alternative investments 175, 192
    charts 80–1, 86
    forecasting 195–6
    fund selection 80–1, 86, 95, 101
    investment trusts 175
    market crisis 202
    Morningstar 75, 81, 92, 95,
      239–42
    portfolios 114, 131
    press relations 220, 226
    research 3, 92, 95
  shares 192–3
  see also websites
Invesco Perpetual High Income 89–90,
  156–7
Invesco Perpetual Tactical Bonds 122,
  128
Investment Association 57–60
investment funds *see* fund investments
investment styles 62, 67–8, 74–6, 80,
  90–1, 111, 237

investment trusts (closed-ended funds)
  5, 40, 42–3, 157
  costs 104
  forecasting 197
  history 40, 42–3
  performance 157–8, 175–83, 194
  websites 51
Investors Chronicle 218
ISA *see* Individual Savings Account

J

Japanese funds
  forecasting 198
  fund investments 87–8
  passive investments 173
  performance 150, 154–5, 159–60, 166
journalists 217–26
Jupiter's Merlin funds 99

K

key takeaways 227–8
Knowledge Management Software 191

L

large-cap companies 76, 90, 167, 239
Legg Mason 87–8
lending rates 19
life expectancy considerations 16
life insurance 9
lifetime allowances 206–7
Lindsell, Michael 159
Lindsell Train Global Equity 73, 123–5,
  128, 147, 159–60
Lipper's professional research 81, 95
Littlewood, William 154
logistics, websites 51–2
long run rates of return 20–3, 25, 34, 37
losses, dealing with 198–203
'low-risk' investments 116–19

lump sum contributions 35–6, 39, 120, 122–3, 141

M

M&G Optimal Income 160–1
M&G unit trusts 41
McClure, John 89–90
Majestic Wine 152–3
management
    companies 72–81, 85–95, 98–108
    costs 101–6
    exchange-traded funds 61
    fund investments 60–3, 66–70, 72–81, 85–95, 98–108
    open-ended funds 61
    portfolios 112–38, 163–7
    unit trusts 61
    venture capital trusts 184–7
manager character/personality considerations 99–101
market confidence 143–6
market crisis 114, 140, 195–203
market scares 144
market sectors
    classification 64
    fund analysis 238–9
    performance 78, 89–93
    portfolios 113–15, 119, 127–8, 132–8
    reports 97
    starting funds 72
    tracking 61–2
Marlborough Multi Cap Income 133, 163
Marlborough small-cap shares 124–5, 147, 152–3, 160–1
Marlborough UK Micro-cap fund 124–5, 147
Marlborough UK Nano-cap fund 147, 163
Marriage, Paul 168–9

Maven venture capital trusts 186
maximising real returns 30, 32
media products 131, 137
media/press relationships 217–26
medium-risk investments 116–17, 122–4, 126–8
meeting investors 92
mergers 80
Merlin funds 99
minimum real returns 32
mining funds 134–6
mixed-asset income 58–9
Mobeus venture capital trusts 186
model portfolio diversification 120–7
Money Management 86
Money Observer 218, 225, 233
MoneyWeek 218, 225–6, 233
Monitise 193
monitoring investments 5
Morgan Grenfell 99
Morningstar website 75, 81, 92, 95, 239–42
mortgages 33, 188
MSCI Europe ex-UK 118
multi-manager fund managers
    fund analysis 243–5
    fund selection 99, 126
    HL Income & Growth Trust 125–6, 144, 146, 148, 163
    number reliability 81
mutual funds 40–3

N

nano-caps 107, 147, 163
Neptune Russia fund 136
net asset values 175–9, 186–7
newspapers
    advertising 215, 217
    dealing with 217–22

newspapers *(cont)*
  fund investments 80–1, 85, 95,
    218–20, 222–9
  press relationships 217–26
  selling financial services 223–4
Newton Asian Income 160–1
Newton Emerging Income 124–5
Newton Real Return 122, 126, 128
Nicholls, Dale 178–9
Nickols, Dan 76, 108–10, 153
Nikkei indices 173
Nimmo, Harry 76, 153
nine-box style matrix classification 75–6
Northern Venture 186
number reliability 81–5, 111

O

OCF *see* ongoing charges figure
Octopus 186
OEIC *see* open-ended investment
  company
offshore funds 56, 59, 172–3, 191
oil sector 133, 136, 193
Old Mutual UK Alpha 123–4, 128, 153
Old Mutual UK Dynamic 167–8
Old Mutual UK Smaller Companies
  fund 108–10
Old Mutual's Small Cap fund 201
on-line platforms *see* websites
one-stop websites *see* websites
ongoing charges figure (OCF) 69,
  103–6, 235
open-ended funds
  costs 104
  history 40–3
  management 61
  problems with 47–50
  unit trusts 42–3
  websites 51

open-ended investment company
  (OEIC)
  costs 104
  history 41–3
  management 61
  problems with 47–9
  unit trusts 42–3
  websites 51
Osborne, George 204
outgoings considerations 15
overseas funds 56, 59, 172–3, 191
owner-managers, fund investments 73

P

paperwork advantages, websites 51
passive investments 60–3, 171–5, 194
  costs 104, 172–3
  performance 171–5, 194
  selection issues 5, 60–3, 69–70
  tracker funds 61, 172–5
past-performance considerations 49, 66,
  78–81, 96–7
patience 107–10, 227
PE of 8 202–3
pensions 2–3, 46, 99
  annual limits 206–7
  annuity 206–8
  costs 141–2
  example investments 139, 141–3,
    146–8, 155, 161–3, 170
  financial plans 211–13
  lifetime allowances 206–7
  need for 203–13
  on-line platforms 51, 53
  performance 139, 142–3, 146–8,
    161–3, 170
  revolution 203–13
  rules and regulations 29
  savings 210–13
  taxes 2, 27–9, 38, 46

pensions *(cont)*
  time considerations 208–10
  viewpoints 24
  websites 51, 53
  see also self-invested personal
    pensions
percentage dividend payments 64
percentage growth rates of returns 20–2,
  188
percentage rate fees 103
performance
  Artemis Strategic Assets 122–3, 126,
    128, 147, 154–6, 168
  bonds 150–2, 154–5, 166
  buy-to-let property 187–90, 194
  cash investments 147, 149, 154
  closed-ended funds 157–8, 175–83
  Darwin Leisure 146, 148–50
  equity income funds 123–5, 128,
    143–8, 154–7, 159–61, 168–70
  fees 104
  fund analysis 233–45
  fund investments 49, 66–9, 74–91,
    96–7, 100–11, 139–70
  gilts/government bonds 150–1, 154
  global equity funds 123–5, 128, 147,
    159–60
  HL Multi-Manager Income &
    Growth Trust 125–6, 144, 146, 148,
    163
  Individual Savings Accounts 139,
    142–3, 146, 160–3, 170
  investment trusts 157–8, 175–83, 194
  Japanese funds 150, 154–5, 159–60,
    166
  Lindsell Train Global Equity 123–5,
    128, 147, 159–60
  Marlborough small-cap shares 124–5,
    147, 152–3
  passive funds 171–5, 194
  personal pensions 139, 142–3, 146–8,
    161–3, 170

portfolios 163–7
property 187–90
RIT Capital Partners 147, 158, 183
Royal London Sterling Extra Yield
  Bond 125–6, 147, 150–2
self-invested personal pensions 139,
  142–3, 146–8, 161–3, 170
shares 190–4
small-cap shares 152–3
specialist products 157, 165
venture capital trusts 139, 146, 183–7,
  194
Woodford Equity Income 123–5, 128,
  144, 146, 156–7
personal finance pressures 222–5
personal pensions
  fund investments 58
  need for 203–13
  performance 139, 142–3, 146–8,
    161–3, 170
  savings 210–13
  tax benefits 2, 27–8
  websites 51, 53
personality considerations 99–101
pharmaceuticals 61, 114, 128, 133, 157
Pidcock, Jason 145
planning basics 13–16
planning investment programmes 31–2
portfolios
  bias issues 121–2
  bonds 116, 118–33, 138
  building and managing 112–38
  cash 119, 126–8, 137–8
  children 125
  corporate bonds 118–19, 128
  costs 132, 161–3
  creation 5, 112–38
  diversification 117–27, 131–4
  dividends 133–5
  equities 114, 119–20, 123–6, 129–32
  example investments 142–9, 155–70

portfolios *(cont)*
    experience considerations 163–5
    fashion 112–15, 138
    financial products 128, 133–4
    fixed-interest securities 116, 118–33, 138
    fund numbers 127–33
    gilts/government bonds 116–19
    government debt 116, 119
    high-risk investments 116–18, 124–6
    income levels 114, 120–8, 131–3
    low-risk investments 116–19
    managing 112–38, 163–7
    market sectors 113–15, 119, 127–8, 132–8
    media products 131, 137
    medium-risk investments 116–17, 122–4, 126–8
    performance 163–7
    property 118–19, 121
    rebalancing 129–33, 138, 161–3
    regular income 125–6
    return rates 113, 115–18, 123–6, 129–34
    risk factors 113–30, 134–8
    Russia 134–7
    selecting investment funds 5
    selling funds 167–9
    shares 118–21, 124, 134
    specialist products 114–15, 128, 131–8
    technology products 114–15, 131–2
    telecommunication products 131
    themes 72, 133–8
    time considerations 132–3, 163–7
    valuation 112–15
    websites 114, 131
    weighting 127–33
potential investment returns 16, 18–23
potential rates of return 16, 18–38
precious metals 155
premium rating charges/fees 69

press relationships 217–26
pressures on personal finance 222–5
price considerations 26–7, 29–30, 33, 36
private pension plans 141, 205
probate issues 52–3
problems with fund investments 46–50
professional skill access 61–3
professional viewpoints 81, 95–7
projecting future returns 32–5
property
    basics of investing 18, 20, 23–5, 30, 32, 34, 37–8
    buy-to-let 5, 24, 187–90, 194
    fund investments 58–60
    investment trusts 158
    performance 187–90
    portfolios 118–19, 121
    rates of return 18, 20, 23–5, 30, 32, 34, 37–8
Provident Financial shares 160–1, 192

Q

quantitative analysis 81, 83–5
quantitative easing 150, 154–5, 221–2
Quindell 193

R

R-squared ratio 242
radio 225
ranking asset classes 25
rates of return 16, 18–38
    bank deposits 19, 28, 36
    bonds 18, 20, 24–5, 33–4, 36–8
    building society deposits 19–20, 23, 28
    cash investments 18–26, 28–9, 31–2, 34–8
    commercial properties 20, 23
    compounding 20–3, 27, 34–5

rates of return *(cont)*
  equities 18, 20, 23–6, 31–2, 34, 36–8
  fixed-interest securities 18, 20, 24–5,
    33–4, 36–8
  gilts/government bonds 20, 23, 25–6,
    31–2
  index-linked gilts 20, 23, 26
  inflation rates 19–26, 30, 34, 38
  long run rates 20–3, 25, 34, 37
  percentage growth rates 20–2
  property 18, 20, 23–5, 30, 32, 34,
    37–8
  residential properties 20, 23
  shares 18, 20, 23–6, 31–2, 34, 36–8
  time considerations 20–3, 26–7,
    31–5, 38
RDR *see* Retail Distribution Review
'real assets' 24
real return rate values 20, 22–4, 26, 30,
  34–5
rebalancing portfolios 129–33, 138, 161–3
reflections on experience 195–226
regional breakdown analysis 165, 237–8
regular contribution investments 27,
  33–4, 37
regular income, portfolios 125–6
regulations/regulators
  advertising 216
  buy-to-let properties 188
  fund investments 48, 66, 78, 85, 98,
    102–3, 141–2
  pensions 29
reinvesting dividends 235
relief rules, taxes 27–9
reporting
  fund investments 78, 81, 85, 93, 97,
    102
  press relationships 217–26
research considerations 71–111, 236–45
  websites 3, 92, 95
residential properties 20, 23

resources companies 134–6
retail banks 214–15
Retail Distribution Review (RDR) 97–8
return rates
  asset classes 18–38
  averages 20, 25–7, 30, 34, 37
  costs 26–7, 29–30, 33, 36
  fund investments 58–9, 63–5, 70, 80
  inflation rates 19–26, 30, 34, 38
  investment trusts 180–1
  portfolios 113, 115–18, 123–6, 129–34
  potential scenarios 16, 18–38
  real values 20, 22–4, 26, 30, 34–5
  risk factors 30–2, 36–7
  taxes 27–30, 34, 38
  venture capital trusts 186
  see also dividends
revolution in pensions 203–13
risk
  advert writing 216
  diversification 117–27
  fund investments 67, 80–1, 102
  gilts/government bonds 116–19
  portfolios 113–30, 134–8
  return rates 30–2, 36–7
RIT Capital Partners 147, 158, 183
Rothschild, Jacob 158
Royal London Sterling Extra Yield Bond
  125–6, 147, 150–2
rules and regulation information 29
runaway inflation 7, 18
Russia 134–7, 145

S

S&P 500 index 172–3
Sanditon 73
savings
  advertising 217
  pensions 210–13

scale, fund investments 44–5

scandals 215–16

Schroder Absolute UK Dynamic fund 168–9

Section 226 schemes 141

selection issues

actively managed funds 60–3, 70

fund investments 5, 47, 56–66, 69–111

passive managed funds 5, 60–3, 69–70

self-invested personal pensions (SIPP) 2, 27–8

performance 139, 142–3, 146–8, 161–3, 170

websites 51, 53

selling funds 167–9

shares 4

basics of investing 18, 20, 23–6, 31–2, 34, 36–8

direct investments 190–4

fund investments 41–5, 51, 58–62, 64–5, 67

Individual Savings Accounts 160–1

internet 192–3

performance 190–4

portfolios 118–21, 124, 134

rates of return 18, 20, 23–6, 31–2, 34, 36–8

websites 51

Sharpe ratio 96, 242

simplicity benefits 10–11, 91–3

SIPP *see* self-invested personal pensions

Sirius Minerals 193

size rankings 165–6

skew 131–2

Slater Investments 203

small-cap shares 76–7, 90, 107, 111, 125, 152–3, 160–1, 168, 201

specialist products

fund investments 56, 58–60, 76, 95, 111, 150, 163, 184–7

market confidence 145–6

performance 157, 165

portfolios 114–15, 128, 131–8

venture capital trusts 186

Square Mile 95

Standard Life 124, 153

standards 102

star rating systems 95–6

statutory reports 93

sterling fund investments 60, 65, 150–2, 155

'stick to the discipline' 93–5

stock lending 173

stock market crash of 1987 114, 140, 195–7

styles of investing 62, 67–8, 74–6, 80, 90–1, 111, 237

Sunday Times 219, 220, 233

surveys, portfolios 113

T

T-bills (cash) 20

tag confusion 65

targeted absolute return products 58

Taube, Nils 100

'tax wrappers' 2, 28

taxes

author's investments 139–40, 142–3, 146, 152, 160–3, 167, 170

basics of investing 16

benefits 2, 5, 27–9, 34, 38, 45–7, 51, 54, 184–6

buy-to-let properties 189–90

dividends 7, 28, 139, 185–6

fund investments 2, 27–9, 38, 45–7, 51–4

importance of avoiding 27–9

pensions 2, 27–9, 38, 46

taxes *(cont)*
    relief rules 27–9
    return rates 27–30, 34, 38
    venture capital trusts 184–6
    websites 52–3
    see also Individual Savings Accounts;
        self-invested personal pensions
technology boom 114–15
technology products 58–9, 114–15, 131–2,
    157, 202
telecommunication products 58–9, 61,
    131
Telegraph 219, 220
television
    advertising 216–17
    press relationships 224–5
ten-bagger shares 191
themes, portfolios 72, 133–8
Thomas, Nigel 202
time considerations
    asset-allocation 164
    fund investments 49–50
    pensions 208–10
    portfolios 132–3, 163–7
    rates of return 20–3, 26–7, 31–5, 38
The Times 220, 233
tobacco sector 114, 157
Topic indices 173
tracker funds 51, 61, 172–5
'tracking errors' 172
tracking market sectors 61–2
trade associations, fund investments
    57–60
Train, Nick 97, 159
traps, fund investments 49–50, 54
Troy Trojan 122
Trustnet 81, 92, 95, 226
Tulloch, Angus 108–10
    UCITS 3 funds 41

U

Unicorn Income 89–90
unit trusts 8–9, 149
    advertising 218
    fund investments 61
    history 40–3
    investment trusts 175, 180–2
    management 61
    OEICs 42–3
    platforms 51
    problems with 47–9
    suitability 212
    websites 51
United Kingdom (UK) listed products
    fund investments 56, 58–67
    performance 148, 152–4, 156–60,
        165–6
United States (USA)
    fund performance 165
    fund selection 77
    passive investments 173
    portfolios 113, 119
    risk 67
unregulated funds 6, 149–50

V

valuation
    importance of 112–15
    portfolios 112–15
value investing 74–6
venture capital trusts (VCT)
    definitions 183
    history 42
    management 184–7
    performance 139, 146, 183–7, 194
    websites 51
Virgin funds 56, 105
volatility
    fund investments 80, 86, 95–6, 111

volatility *(cont)*
    portfolios 115–16

W

websites 2
    access issues 51–3
    addresses 226, 232–3
    administration advantages 51–4
    alternative investments 175, 192
    benefits of 51–3
    charts 80–1, 86
    costs 51–2
    financial press relations 220, 226
    forecasting 195–6
    fund analysis 235–7
    fund investments 50–4, 59–60
        alternative investments 175, 192
        charts 80–1, 86
        financial press relations 220, 226
        forecasting 195–6
        fund selection 80–1, 86, 95, 101
        investment trusts 175
        market crisis 202
        Morningstar 75, 81, 92, 95,
            239–42
        portfolios 114, 131
        research 3, 92, 95
    fund selection 80–1, 86, 95, 101
    Individual Savings Accounts 51
    Investment Association 59–60
    investment trusts 51, 175
    logistics 51–2
    market crisis 202
    Morningstar 75, 81, 92, 95, 239–42
    OEICs 51
    pensions 51, 53
    portfolios 114, 131
    probate issues 52–3
    research 3, 92, 95

self-invested personal pensions 51, 53
    shares 51
    tax benefits 52–3
    taxes 52–3
    tracker funds 51
    unit trusts 51
    useful addresses 226, 232–3
    venture capital trusts 51
    see also internet
weighting
    investment styles 75–6
    portfolios 127–33
Woodford Equity Income 123–5, 128,
    144, 146, 156–7
Woodford Investment Management 73
Woodford, Neil 73, 89, 91, 97, 144,
    156–7, 161, 181, 202
Woodford Patient Capital Trust 104, 157,
    160–1
Woolnough, Richard 156, 161
worst-case scenario planning 199–200

Y

yields
    bonds 150–2, 154–5
    buy-to-let properties 188–90
    gilts/government bonds 150–1, 154

Z

zero-sum game 63
Zoopla 186

THANKS
FOR READING!

Our readers mean everything to us at Harriman House. As a special thank-you for buying this book let us help you save as much as possible on your next read:

If you've never ordered from us before, get £5 off your first order at **harriman-house.com** with this code: `eifne55`

Already a customer? Get £5 off an order of £25 or more with this code: `44dmdeii`

Get 7 days' FREE access to hundreds of our books at **volow.co** – simply head over and sign up.

Thanks again!
from the team at

CPSIA information can be obtained at www.ICGtesting.com
Printed in the USA
BVOW06s0704201215

430666BV00026B/286/P

9 780857 194671